BEYOND the DAYS of the GIANTS

Solving the Crisis of Growth and Succession in Today's CPA Firms

BEYOND the DAYS of the GIANTS

Solving the Crisis of Growth and Succession in Today's CPA Firms

Paul D. Fisher

CRC Press
Taylor & Francis Group
Boca Raton   London   New York

CRC Press is an imprint of the
Taylor & Francis Group, an **informa** business

A PRODUCTIVITY PRESS BOOK

CRC Press
Taylor & Francis Group
6000 Broken Sound Parkway NW, Suite 300
Boca Raton, FL 33487-2742

Printed on acid-free paper
Version Date: 20130822

International Standard Book Number-13: 978-1-4822-0356-1 (Paperback)

Visit the Taylor & Francis Web site at
http://www.taylorandfrancis.com

and the CRC Press Web site at
http://www.crcpress.com

For my dearest Colleen, who worked so hard
while she waited for me to grow up.

I'm glad you got a glimpse of our shared legacy.
I promise to keep growing it for us.

Contents

Foreword

The themes today in accounting firms are often the themes of yesterday. However, today is different and the profession has changed. Clients are more sophisticated and demanding, partners are retiring at an alarming rate, and many younger practitioners are fleeing the profession.

I am old enough to remember the Days of the Giants and was fortunate to live through those exciting times as a young partner in an aggressive accounting firm in Chicago. I witnessed firsthand the way the Giants operated. I was on the scene to watch the up-or-out policies of firms and the traditional pyramid structure with partners at the top enjoying the "good life" while staff accountants at the bottom labored diligently to move up the pyramid. If you were going to remain in the profession, you had one goal—to become a partner.

Today, managing partners struggle to get partners committed to the firm, to keep them accountable, and to figure out how to pass the firm to the next generation of owners, if they are fortunate enough to have that next generation.

As a result, the Days of the Giants are slowing fading away. Clients are more sophisticated and demanding, the practitioners' pool is shrinking, and more and more firms vie for the same clients—competing on price rather than differentiation. Firms are struggling to find new ways to create value for clients, to engage younger professionals to take over, and to solve the succession issues a majority of CPA firms currently face.

Against this background, Paul Fisher presents a compelling case that enables firms today to meet the future, engage the next generation of owners, and create value for today's clients. While you may not agree with everything in the book, I can assure you Paul Fisher will challenge you to think. And, that is what a great book is all about!

In the last thirty years, the approach to client services has changed in all professional service firms. Clients have also changed dramatically. Whereas thirty years ago, they considered the service provider as all-knowing, today they are partners with service providers. In addition, clients were not as knowledgeable about our services as they are today. Professional service firms have spent millions of dollars educating clients about their services and how best to use them via their marketing efforts.

As with virtually everything from magazines and sport shoes to professional services, buyers seek niche products and services. Go to any bookstore and look at the number of magazines under any genre. The days of the generic "gym shoe" are long gone. In the professional service arena, the focus is on specialization. While the generalist knew a little about a lot, today's specialist knows a lot about a small or even micro area.

Who then coordinates all the services that a firm can bring to its clients in order to create the most value to the client? Fisher takes us through the Mayo Clinic model as one solution to this question. While some of the more advanced firms have already figured out the answer to this question, many firms need to move beyond being client focused to ultimately becoming the client's preferred and trusted advisor.

I suggest that your get your colored highlighter out and start reading this well-written and practical book. You won't be disappointed. I know I wasn't.

* * *

August Aquila is an internationally known consultant to professional service firms and the author of several books on managing and leading professional service firms.

Acknowledgments

The process of writing this book started over a decade ago as I concluded that my profession's succession systems wouldn't survive another repetition. And I was the person at my office responsible for that looming failure. Those were painful times as I struggled to cheerlead the troops, plead for consensus, bark orders—anything I could think of to continue practitioner succession as we'd known it. I had to find a better way to lead my colleagues to the high ground they deserved.

So I began writing—terribly at first—about what it would take to revive the Days of the Giants. Our authoring team's effort gained traction after I accepted the wise advice of my coach, Laurie Harper, to stop trying to impress my audience with what I knew, and to start trying to help them solve their problems. And my editor, Marge Melby, was relentless in reminding me that constructing a good narrative involved a lot more than writing piles of really good sentences.

However, the real story of the book isn't one of self-congratulation but one of gratitude and humility. Hundreds of thousands of CPAs have the same experience, intellectual capacity, and concern for their colleagues as I do. Yet I was the one who wrote this book—and that was no accident. Although I was standing there in the same position as everyone else, when my number was called—and when I had to dig deeper—the raw material was there, thanks to what I'd received from others throughout my life.

I'd started my journey expecting it to bear the fruit of a gift from me to my profession. But it became more about my gratitude for the gifts I'd received—from my ancestors for talents that I hadn't earned, from my siblings for our family culture of literacy to which I'd contributed little, and from my colleagues and our clients whose challenges fueled my passion.

Thank you for those things. I will always use them wisely and in the service of others—as you gave them to me.

We did it, Pat.

Introduction

I don't need to tell the good folks responsible for molding the future of the accounting profession that we're in the middle of a succession crisis. In fact, we're on the brink of a time our profession has never seen. It's estimated that between 40 and 50 percent of all accounting firm partners will retire within the next ten years. In short, there simply aren't near enough younger accountants to turn the car keys over to.

Traditionally, accounting firms relied on as high as ten-to-one staff-to-partner ratios to maintain the profitability needed to keep our ownership systems intact. But after the latest economic decline, with its loss of labor leverage, we know that adequate owner profitability won't be coming back unless we devise new ways to offer far more value with far fewer CPAs.

And partner groups continue to wrestle with what some see as a lack of commitment to the profession by younger accountants. While those groups have been trying to obtain that commitment for quite some time now, they still aren't sure they can confidently turn over the practice car keys to next-generation practitioners, even if they *were* inclined to pick up the keys and drive the car.

At the same time, the rise of process theory and practice in the face of a shrinking and specializing practitioner population has made it pretty clear that our successors won't be able to drive that practice car in the same way their predecessors did. It's likely, in fact, that substantial redesign of that practice vehicle might be necessary to provide for the value-creation capabilities needed to keep our succession systems viable. But what the practice might look like in the future is less than clear.

My research journey for this book began with my own perceptions of the looming crisis, based on my twenty-seven years working as a tax professional and sometime consultant in my own accounting firm. My first writing effort, then, came solely from that somewhat myopic view of our profession, and it earned me a caustic—and wise—response from my authoring coach.

She said that I seemed to be trying to tell people about problems they didn't know they had. My first job as an author, it turns out, is to convince readers that I have answers to problems they're consciously aware of, concerned about, and actively trying to solve.

Having been properly dethroned from my perch atop Mount Smarty-Pants, I refocused my research to the near-retiree baby boomers and their next-in-line successors for guidance. It seemed an improbable route to take at first. If our practitioners knew the nature of their succession problems, I reasoned, surely they'd reverse course and take us quickly and painlessly back to the halcyon days of public accounting. But my coach convinced me to find out what those accountants were thinking before I presumed to try to help them. It was the best advice I've ever gotten.

As it turns out, the retiring practitioners I spoke with know perfectly well what's happened to them as a group. All I needed to do was ask. They're well aware of what they could provide under the circumstances in which they worked, and they know the struggles that younger accountants will be facing under their own set of working conditions. And they sounded many similar themes, one of which was a longing for the days when "real" client service, hard work, and dedication meant something. They'd spent their professional lives working in what I call the "Days of the Giants," an expression I've adopted from a Minnesota Public Radio program I'd heard that talked about similar transitional problems plaguing the medical profession.

The practitioners I spoke with—our "Giants" in this book—had much to say. When I summarized their comments, it became clear that the primary deficit they'll leave behind is a *value-creation crisis*. And they suggested that the professional commitment of their successors—on the wane for some time now—will not rise to a level that will help carry them through to that new world of practice. So we can add a *commitment crisis* to the list of challenges.

Perhaps most interestingly, our Giants were all keenly aware that *not* addressing these problems will threaten not only our firms' equity systems, but also the accounting profession's very growth and relevance.

The accounting profession, of course, isn't the only one struggling to redefine its goals in a changing economic world. Dr. Nicholas LaRusso, director of the Mayo Clinic's Center for Innovation, said it well in an April 2011 presentation of the MPR News *Bright Ideas* series on Minnesota Public Radio. His disarmingly simple mission statement for the medical profession said essentially that it should provide *more services* to *more people, more valuably*, and at a *declining cost*. Such a simple goal as "curing the sick" is surely well served by such an equally simple, yet powerful, mission statement.

As I looked at Dr. LaRusso's observation, I picked it apart as any problem-solving accountant would. Our larger firms addressed the *more services* aspect of his statement with horizontal acquisition of all sorts of ancillary and allied services. Those firms targeted small, specialty practices for purchase so they could acquire services that would differentiate them in the marketplace. Breadth-of-service offerings were going to be the leverage savior.

And to provide that expanded body of services to *more people,* firms had aggressively begun serious marketing and sales efforts quite some time ago. As productivity demands on our CPA specialist practitioners grew, we responded by getting them the sales, marketing, and business-generation help they needed. Our specialists' needs for more procedural work matched up nicely with the efforts of equally highly trained sales professionals who could focus on finding and delivering more procedures to our trusted experts.

While competition among accounting firms had forced them to begin addressing *declining costs,* the single biggest driver of cost was an economic phenomenon called *allocative efficiency.* The accounting function has shrunk as a percentage of total gross domestic product in our economy from something like 5 percent to less than 1 percent of revenues over the last fifty years.

Now, since the 2002 Sarbanes–Oxley Act requires that publicly traded companies be made more transparent, an even more important resource reallocation has begun. Dollars are being taken away from our traditional busy seasons that surround periodic earnings and are being reinvested in creating processes that will help stakeholders throughout the United States and around the globe to more effectively, and dynamically, assess the health of business. Whatever the mechanisms, though, declining *prices* have not been hard for us to accomplish in the recent past. Declining costs, of course, is another story.

Yet I struggled to translate the *more valuably* aspect of Dr. LaRusso's mission statement to the accounting profession. While our economy was clearly demanding specialization, it seemed that our response to that demand was hampering our ability to expand our deliverables and knit them together more valuably. In short, our services were becoming commodities. And I couldn't describe anything I'd seen or heard in my own management activities that addressed it.

So under the wise guidance of our Giants, I set out to find out why. What I learned was that we've done nothing less than methodically and purposefully disassemble the value-creation systems of the retiring generation. We've done so by overresponding to the market constraints of specialization and unit-of-output productivity. At the same time, we've underresponded to the market's inherent demand for value. To be fair, though, the value-creation systems of our Giants needed to be taken apart. They were horribly inefficient and would never work in the growing world of functional specialization coupled with an increasing demand for value. But for us to arrive successfully at the other end of the next decade with our firms intact and our profession growing, we'll need to deal consciously and deliberately with this value-creation crisis and work our way back out of it.

The good news is that if we're successful, the accounting profession will not only survive, but will be poised to move into our natural position as the repository of the value-creation infrastructure of the world economy. But before we can build and maintain that value-management engine for society, we'll first need to prove we can build it for ourselves. Doing so will not just get us safely and quietly to *after* the Days of the Giants, but propel us boldly *beyond* them.

About the Author

Paul Fisher's career in business had its organic beginnings in his lead-guitar-playing, singing, and fry-cooking days in that hotbed of a cultural maelstrom that was Western Wisconsin in the 1970s. He eventually graduated with a degree in accounting from the University of Wisconsin–Eau Claire in 1984 and, inexplicably to some, found employment as a CPA, eventually migrating to the Twin Cities in 1989.

Paul spent the next twenty-two years in public accounting practice there. Along the way, he was bought and sold, merged, and generally reorganized so many times that he considered having barcode installed on his forehead to facilitate the continuous vertical integration exercises. In order to bring stability to his professional life, he organized the Metro Firm Leadership Group, a best-practices consortium made up of Twin Cities Metro Area CPA firms currently representing over 1,000 employees.

In 2011, Paul left his practice in order to write his first book and form New Giants Consulting, an organization dedicated to building the value-creation capabilities of our New Giants.

Chapter 1

The Days of the Giants

I was listening to a radio program one day about the challenges of modern medical practice. The show's guest was Dr. Danielle Ofri, an internist at Bellevue Hospital in New York and editor-in-chief of the *Bellevue Literary Review*. The discussion topic was her July 2011 article, "Why Would Anyone Choose to Become a Doctor?" The interviewer asked Dr. Ofri to explain a reference in that article to "the Days of the Giants."

Dr. Ofri's response was that it was an industry term-of-art describing the feelings of senior and retired doctors about themselves and their practices compared with those of their junior colleagues.* I was stunned to hear her describe what I could easily have heard from my own peers in the accounting profession. The older doctors felt they'd treated patients with a dedication and intelligence that today's less-committed junior colleagues don't. While the senior doctors worked 36- and 48-hour shifts, for example, their junior colleagues were "mere technicians" who wanted to leave the office at 5 p.m. every day. The senior doctors felt they'd worked in the days of the true clinicians. They were the *real* doctors—the "Giants" of the medical profession.

My initial response was the same as Dr. Ofri's. Such comments at first seemed to be those of "jaded has-beens…pining away for the nonexistent Days of the Giants." We baby boomers, like generations before us, fall easily into glowing thoughts of the days of our youth. We were young, ambitious, and weaving the fabric of the careers that would define us not only as professionals, but quite literally as human beings. It's only natural to compare the warm, gauzy images of those days of empire building to what we

---

* Ofri, Danielle. "Why Would Anyone Choose to Become a Doctor?" *New York Times Well Blog*, July 21, 2011. http://well.blogs.nytimes.com/2011/07/21/why-would-anyone-choose-to-become-a-doctor/.

face today as we assess our younger practitioner-successors. It's normal to yearn for simpler days when we had more energy, felt successful, and were growing.

I recall feeling intimidated in college when our department head described how competitive public accounting was. He said that only 2 percent of accounting graduates hiring on at the national firms of that time would make partner some day. While he didn't say it out loud, the other 98 percent who took their basic training in public accounting and then left for industry—as we virtually all did—would somehow be lesser beings than those exalted few.

So public accounting was a bustling, competitive place. Large numbers of new college graduates got their CPA certificates and lined up behind their senior colleagues for the very slim chance of making partner. Only the best and the brightest did, of course, and they were counted among the industry's elite. They would become one of the Giants.

As the retiring generation, we know we'll soon lose that status. We'll lose the mission we served every day at the office. While we hope to let go gracefully, it's uncomfortable to know it will be someone else's turn soon. But it's even more uncomfortable to think that the tools and means of the mission itself might be changing.

It's horrifying. It runs counter to everything we want to believe about ourselves and our legacies. We want the exclamation point on our careers to be, "Good job!" and "Mission accomplished!" We retiring accountants feel that the mission we served *mattered*. Why would we need a new one, for God's sake? When our clients asked for something, damn it, we figured out a way to get it for them. Now. Our young counterparts, we reason, lack the drive, creativity, and work ethic to do what we did. And clients today don't even know whom to call at the firm. Ours were the days of *real* client service. We were the Giants of the accounting profession.

So to hear Dr. Ofri talk of medical practitioners having the same monologue with themselves about their glory days struck me as possibly revealing. Was the common thread simple human yearning for youth? Or was there any substance underlying those beliefs? If so, could we examine them and find our way through the succession crisis dogging our industry? Or was it a silly exercise in the false grandiosity of old men?

I decided it was critical to see if there were common threads of truth to the retiring accountants' complaints about the professional capabilities of our younger counterparts. And if there were, could I piece those threads together in a way that would guide us toward the professional growth we so desperately need to comfortably honor our financial obligations to retiring partners?

The Giants' Laments

In the process of finding an answer to that question, in the fall of 2011, I interviewed colleagues near retirement about their perceptions of the capabilities of the next generation. I came up with a list of what I call the "Giants' Laments"—simple expressions of how those retirement-age CPAs felt they differed from their successors. While I expected a complex variety of "laments," I was surprised instead to find that each fell quite neatly into two major parts of the problem: one of value creation and one of commitment:

Value creation includes these major aspects:

- We were well rounded.
- We knew our clients' unique needs.
- We provided value to clients.
- We were real problem solvers.

Commitment includes these major aspects:

- We were more dedicated to our professional mission.
- We were more entrepreneurial.
- We were more committed to the firm.
- We were accountable to the firm's partners.

Value Creation

One of my colleagues described the value-creation problem in very practical terms. I'd asked him about his biggest fear with respect to the succession crisis, and he told a story of a senior colleague I'll call John, who did all of his own work, especially consulting. My colleague worried that after John retired, his clients would leave the firm because they'd never worked with anyone else there.

We can call this *single-point-of-failure risk*, a term used in the 1960s to describe an engineering flaw that rocket scientists of the day wanted to avoid. All systems needed multiple backups to minimize possible mission failure. We accountants didn't have to worry about such risk in the past, when we had lots of inexpensive, generally skilled CPA labor to pass that knowledge on. But now John's behavior—previously seen as the dedicated commitment to customer service worthy of a Giant—was putting the firm at financial risk. In short, because unit-of-output productivity had severely reduced the firm's number of accountants, John was actually hurting the firm by presenting himself as the creator of all value coming out of it.

So our Giants are correct about the value-creation crisis. Their system of creating value, though—however effective it was in their day—would be wholly inadequate to serve the next generation because now, even if we *could* transfer that single-point-of-failure role from a Giant to a New Giant, there would still be far too few of the latter to create an equivalent amount of value. And that spells trouble for our retirement systems.

Commitment

It's been said of baby boomers that we're somewhat unique in defining ourselves by our work. At times, we paid a high price for that by neglecting other parts of life. While we might wish we could have a "redo" of some of those parts, the truth is we didn't start out wanting to define ourselves by our work. In fact, our youth was a time when we wanted to do quite the opposite—we wanted to define our work by our lives. This need is at the core of idealism, and it's an important lesson in our quest to motivate the next generation. They'll need a mission befitting of, and responsive to, the challenges and opportunities presented to them in their own practice days.

But despite their relative lack of success in solving the succession crisis, the Giants had very accurately nailed its two distinct parts—value creation and commitment—so I began to think about how I might help. Maybe I could design a two-track consulting and coaching system, one to increase firms' abilities to serve clients more valuably, and another to increase practitioner interest in committing to doing it as a career choice.

Yet I wasn't sure if I had a clear enough vision of how the crisis had come about, which seems critical to solving it. During the last ten or fifteen years, we've spent a whole lot of time and money to develop plans for young accountants—and the equivalent of primal scream therapy for our senior partners. Yet here we are a couple of decades later standing at the brink of a succession crisis. With such a modest success rate of our past efforts, it struck me that rather than treat both commitment and value creation separately, we should first think about how those two crises might be interconnected. And perhaps they were interconnected in a causal way that hadn't yet occurred to us.

The stakes involved in solving the combined value-creation and commitment crises that together make up the succession crisis couldn't be much higher. Profits have begun to dry up just as the population of retirees is expected to balloon. The CPA labor leverage we've traditionally relied on to provide the profitability that funded our retirement commitments is gone now, taken from us gradually at first, as technology increased our unit-of-output productivity. Then it suddenly disappeared into thin air as the Great Recession and its productivity demands robbed us of the last vestiges of labor pyramid power—that small stockpile of CPAs we were so carefully nursing to keep our retirement systems afloat.

Profit Management by Tradition

If value creation and commitment aren't solved in the near term, there are all sorts of sound, tried-and-true cost-management options we can employ to reduce the profitability strain of the coming financial shortfall. These traditional options might work to sustain profits, at least in the short term, as we figure out our value-creation and commitment problems.

Hope for the Return of the Business Cycle

First, we can hope that the return of the business cycle brings our prices back up to prerecession levels. But no one's certain if and when that might happen. Commentators on economic growth—who once estimated recovery in quarters and then in one- and two-year increments—now routinely admit that it might be more than a decade before real productivity returns us to our former standard of living and, more pointedly, to expectations for our firms' partner groups. A possibly decade-long process of waiting for the return of the business cycle could leave many of our firms without the means to fund our retirement systems in the interim.

Find Forms of Less Expensive Labor

Firms can begin to replace CPAs with less costly labor to reduce production costs of core offerings. If firms are careful in their internal training and systems development, there's likely some opportunity here. Unfortunately, fewer CPAs in the face of increased specialization only makes the value-creation problem worse. As client duties move from very many generally skilled retirees to very few specialist-trained successors, our value-creation capability will teeter under the strain. We need more CPAs, not fewer, to create maximum financial leverage.

Find New Ancillary Services

Firms can bring new technology, financial services, human capital systems, and other consulting products on board to shore up the revenues necessary to help maintain top-line volume. Depending on your ability to horizontally integrate those offerings, you might thus get some overhead contribution. Unfortunately, the Great Recession seems to be putting as much, or probably more, pricing stress on those allied products and services as it is on our core offerings.

As that price pressure stiffens, not only will it be tougher to compete with non-CPA-firm providers of the same ancillary services, but your main fight might ultimately be defending against *their* horizontal migration toward *your* core offerings. You could then face not just the challenge of slow growth, but one of severely reduced revenue when competitors arrive at your clients' doorstep ready to integrate your ancillary services into their infrastructure offerings.

Decide to Merge

Last, of course, you can merge. As I write this book, significant lateral mergers—or mergers of equals—have already occurred in the top twenty-five US firms, and we can expect that trend to continue in the top four hundred firms as they look for ways to reduce costs. The accounting industry has traditionally used mergers of smaller specialty firms for strategic horizontal growth. While firms might declare the current wave of mergers to be strategic—and all about increased breadth-of-service offerings and industries served—it's pretty clearly more related to the need to have our administrative and leadership resources serve larger gross margins. As good accountants, we want to reduce our fixed costs.

Unfortunately, the industry's profit expectations from mergers will be problematic at best. The political pressure to retain managers from each merger participant, along with the fact that fixed costs are only *partially* fixed, usually means a savings that is considerably less than 100 percent for one set of premerger administrative costs. So if you've never been part of a lateral merger, you might want to consult some of your colleagues who have. Your expectations for cost savings will then be more realistic.

But rather than look to old cost-management ways to solve the new problems caused by the value-creation and commitment deficits, we might more profitably try to unwind the real causes of the crisis that our Giants spelled out for us. In the process, we'll be able to decide what actions to take and in what sequence to take them. If we don't specifically plan for that, we risk treating symptoms, not causes, of our problem.

So first, let's consider the following simple analogy to clarify and depersonalize discussion of the value-creation and commitment crises.

The Keys or the Car?

I decided it might be helpful to think of the succession crisis as a car. On one side are the retiring practitioners (drivers) who expect to some day very soon hand over the keys to the car to the guys on the other side, their successors (student drivers). So I asked my research participants if they could quantify how much of the succession crisis was caused by three things:

1. The inability or unwillingness (commitment) of retiring practitioners to hand over the (value-creation) keys to the car
2. The inability or unwillingness (commitment) of the student drivers to take the (value-creation) keys to the car and drive it
3. The need for a new (value-creation) car to more effectively engage the successor practitioner (commitment)

Invariably, the practitioners' age dictated their response. My retiring research participants were acutely aware of the value-creation problem, but they assigned a much higher percentage of its cause to the unwillingness or inability of their junior practitioners to take the value-creation keys to the car. They felt that the biggest loss when they retired would be their special knowledge base of each unique client need. And they worried that not enough of the younger practitioners would commit long enough to assimilate all the knowledge they'd employed to create value with their clients.

That knowledge—all those bits of minutiae that used to add up to competitive business advantage—is now becoming a liability, because there aren't nearly enough people to carry it forward. Now, way fewer CPAs are far more preoccupied with tax returns and audits than they are with the unique client aches and pains, where a lot of value resides.

In the minds of the older practitioners, the real core of the succession crisis was a commitment problem caused by voluntary, self-induced generational differences and not competing market constraints. We reasoned that the next generation had never lived through a war, experienced serious social upheaval, or had to fend for themselves in any compelling way. They were coddled by us, their baby-boomer parents, who sought to shelter them from life's challenges by making sure they always had the best schools, activities, and social connections. We wanted advantages for our children that we'd never had. And now we thought we'd spoiled them. They weren't committing to us and our clients, we reasoned, because we'd bred it out of them with their privileged upbringing.

For the junior practitioners of my research, the resounding message was also that—first and foremost—there was a commitment problem. But they described the core problem of senior colleagues as "resistance to change." This posed another challenge to my wanting to be rigorous about the cause of the crisis. I'm naturally suspicious of easy, culturally oriented excuses for relationship conflict. Listen, for example, to a young colleague's description of the nature of her senior colleagues' criticism of junior accountants:

> We have all sorts of engagement letters with legal language and [IRC section] 7216 letters…that just slow things down and get in the way of just helping the client. They do a lot of [complaining] that checklists, etc., make something that should take 30 minutes take 5 hours. They don't see the speed in young people that they think should be there.

To me that doesn't sound like an old-fashioned resistance to change or an inability to react to procedural quality constraints. After all, senior management developed all of the related paperwork used in practice today. All the junior colleagues can control is how fast they work. The senior colleagues are simply hurting because they've hit the intrinsic value cap of what they're providing to the client. To view the risk-management materials as "getting in the way of just helping the client" is the same as saying they're struggling with the same value-creation crisis that our Giants told us about. The only "change" they're "resisting" is that they'll need to send a bigger bill to the clients and thus risk losing them.

History always reminds us that each generation disappoints its predecessors in important ways, but that we manage to "continue the brand" in spite of it. There's no mystery there. A cottage industry has arisen in the study of generational differences. The hope is that if we can understand one another's different values and goals that it will be (1) easier for the Giants to commit to turning over the car keys to their junior colleagues and (2) more likely that they'll be more willing to take those keys from the Giants for their turn at the wheel.

It began to strike me that maybe the causal relationship was upside down in these exercises. Generations probably don't see themselves differently than their elders and then go about wreaking havoc on last year's socioeconomic and political systems in a narcissistic attempt to make them reflect their own cultural needs. It's quite the reverse, really. *Generations differ in values and capabilities because they face different challenges.* Socioeconomic response to those compelling and unavoidable constraints is what drives differing values and culture. We eventually get exactly what we ask from them.

Think for a moment about Tom Brokaw's book, *The Greatest Generation.**
The folks who suffered through the Great Depression and World War II accomplished greatness under adversity unimaginable by Americans today. That generation produced an unprecedented number of great generals, statesmen, and empire-building entrepreneurs. We could say, "What luck! Imagine the coincidence of that particular generation producing just the right people at just the right time!" It's a silly exercise but illustrates that society produces what it needs based on the socioeconomic realities of the day. And that's exactly what's happening in the accounting profession.

So our senior, near-retirement CPA Giants tell me that the value-creation system of their firms is at risk because they don't have the commitment necessary from the next generation to keep it afloat. But our junior colleagues tell me that they don't see the commitment they need from the retiring generation to adapt to changes brought by specialization and technology. Both sides of that generational "war" wanted to characterize commitment as their primary succession problem. They were telling me, in effect, that if we solve the commitment problem, the value-creation problem will automatically resolve itself.

There was surprisingly little belief that option number three in our multiple-choice test—the design and operation of the value-creation systems themselves, or "the car"—had a lot to do with succession ineffectiveness. And this belief is clearly reflected in traditional accounting firm investment policy in training and development. Most expenditures for firm development

---

* Brokaw, Tom. *The Greatest Generation*. New York: Dell Publishing, 1998.

that are unrelated to subject matter are geared toward either encouraging commitment on one or both sides of the succession aisle, or training successors in the soft skills of communications, leadership, and selling abilities that were bred out of them during their specialist training.

But the more I talked to practitioners, firm managers, and consultants in our profession, the more I came to believe that we might have the causal relationship backward. That is, rather than our having a commitment problem that's causing a value-creation deficit, we have a value-creation problem that's causing a decline in practitioner commitment.

No, lack of ability and commitment of our younger accountants is not our *first* problem. Nor is our first problem prying the car keys from the reluctant fingers of our near-retirees. It's not in training back into younger CPAs what we've relentlessly bred out of them. They've become the experts and specialists we asked them to be. Having more of them commit so that we have the CPA leverage we used to have to sustain our retirement systems doesn't solve the problem either. We'd only see their increased charges in nonbillable works-in-progress and have an even *bigger* value-creation problem. So, it's pretty clear that practitioner-to-practitioner commitment won't help until we figure out how to use our CPAs more valuably than we have in the past.

So, if our crisis is not caused by our successors' lack of commitment, then what is preventing them from picking up the value-creation keys to the car and getting on with the road trip? The quick answer, and the subject of this book, is that the underlying value-creation crisis is not about who's holding the keys to the car. In fact, *it isn't about the keys at all but about the car itself.*

We don't need that new value-creation car to please willful and misguided children who've been pampered and are thus less committed. Rather, our successors need their own sense of mission because today's social, economic, and political conditions demand it. Rallying around those demands will drive them to pursue goals they'll need to accomplish their mission together, just like the Giants did. And despite the fact that the mission is exactly the same as it always was—protect the public interest—the market is forcing our successors to dramatically change the way they'll accomplish it.

It's vital, then, that we focus on the forces being unleashed on our successors in the post–Great Recession era. Understanding those forces will tell us exactly where to apply the resources to bring back the business leverage that will keep our retirement systems flourishing. We have to get on with the task of building a new value-creation system for what will be the Days of the *New* Giants. And we need to start the process *right now* if we're to survive as a thriving and relevant profession.

So, while we don't need to worry about practitioner-to-practitioner commitment just yet, it will be *critical* down the road. Junior practitioners want to look up to their senior colleagues. They want to feel as though they're joined with them in pursuit of a holy mission. And we desperately need a new value-creation car to drive along the highway of that mission to inspire that commitment.

But before asking practitioners to commit to one another, before venturing into the Days of the New Giants, firms will first need to make *three other important commitments*—not from practitioner to practitioner—but *from our firms to the marketplace.* That is, we must commit to:

1. Practitioner-led value creation
2. Consumer-defined quality
3. Our new professional mission

But before we lay the bedrock for those market promises, it's critical that we first come to understand how we arrived in this particular place at this particular time. We need to own up to the problem we've created and to recognize that value creation has to occur differently now. And we need to accept that it's our personal responsibility to deal with it. There are no more generations left to defer that challenge to. Only then can we begin building the road map to our new value-creation infrastructure and secure the future for our *New* Giants.

Chapter 2

Giants and Dinosaurs

It's no longer news that we can't restore the succession systems of the Days of the Giants. We've been trying that unsuccessfully for a couple of decades now, with little success. Over the years, we made sure that younger CPAs were adequately paid. We increased diversity, embraced sustainability, held our tongues politically, and limited the number of hours we asked them to work. Yet we're still in a crisis, and there's been little discussion of what to do about it, other than trying to obtain their commitment by making it easier to stay. What it might take to make them *want* to stay, despite a challenging environment, has been largely unspoken or, at best, only vaguely referred to.

So how did we get where we are today from the Days of the Giants? Why does making a living have to be so much harder these days? Why are our services "commodities" now? And, by the way, *who did this to us?*

Let's answer the last question first. We did this to ourselves. Typically, when I listen to colleagues talking about our core services, they say things like, "Our clients don't value us the way that they used to," or "Our services have become commodities." The first statement blames our clients, and the second one blames the products themselves. Admitting blame is hard work. But the need for us to accept responsibility for what our services have become is not a breast-beating or self-recognition exercise. Only if we admit that the choices we made to turn our services into commodities were ours alone can we make different choices tomorrow and start reversing that trend.

The story of how we systematically disassembled the value-creation systems of the Giants is a cautionary one. It's important to understand how that happened. While it's true that our value-creation systems have gone the way of the dinosaurs, those systems were crucial to industry growth back then.

And just because our old value-creation system became fatally inefficient doesn't mean we don't need a functioning one today.

Our Giants are dead-on correct about our value-creation crisis. And they're right when they say that their successors don't have the same drive, creativity, and work ethic. But what they didn't tell us is that *those combined attributes were provided by a minimum of three different people* in the Days of the Giants. Value-creation systems in their day were populated by unique races of dinosaurs traditionally known in consulting as Finders, Minders, and Grinders. And together they provided the drive, creativity, and work ethic that made up the mythical Giant they all imagined themselves to be.

> **Finders.** Our Finders were the rainmakers. They provided the drive to generate new work. When they walked into a room, they were looking for nothing more than what was needed by whoever happened to be in the room. They were inspiring "promisers of stuff." The sky was the limit, at a price you could afford. You need it, we'll figure out how to get it for you. Available labor was cheap and generally skilled, so our Finders' work was fairly easy.
>
> **Minders.** The Minders were the creative folks in the muddy business of trying to keep Finders' promises to clients. They were the equivalent of the design thinkers of today in business process engineering. They were team-oriented, end-user-focused people who did their best to guide a firm's build-to-suit, value-creation efforts. They oversaw the horizontal integration of all specialist, or Grinder, functions that produced an outcome-based result.
>
> **Grinders.** The Grinders provided the work ethic and problem-solving skills that got the work done. These folks did most of the heavy lifting in terms of the work required to deliver the value that the Finders promised and the Minders engineered. They'd typically work 3,000 hours or more per year but only report 2,300 to keep their billable charges down, which of course masked the growing sustainability problem inside their increasingly expensive value-creation system.

Glory Days

The days of CPA practice before the age of specialization were an opportunity wonderland. If you were bright, willing to work hard, and politically astute enough to align yourself with a powerful firm partner, client, or other patron, there was little to stop you from succeeding. You just needed to work the system hard and long enough to make it. There were few entry barriers other than needing to get one's CPA certificate to practice. I recall that, back in the 1980s, there were still some state boards of accountancy that didn't even require an accounting degree to sit for the uniform CPA exam.

To illustrate the Wild West mentality of the day, one of our Giants told me a story of a particularly stubborn and powerful rainmaker-partner who decided that he was going to mentor an employee he'd found in the "secretarial pool." The partner was getting fed up with the relatively harder-to-manage accounting college graduates he worked with and—very much like the Giants today—wanted nothing more than to have smart subordinates who'd simply do what he asked them to do, when he asked them to do it. So—with nothing more than a high school diploma, hard work, and a fierce loyalty to her benefactor—that chosen successor rose from secretary to the rank of audit partner with the New York office of the sponsoring partner's national firm.

That story, as unlikely as it was back then, couldn't happen today. Today, our undergraduate degree programs are criticized for a lack of diversity and well-roundedness. Yet, at the same time, those programs are panned as being inadequate technical preparation for promotion beyond a senior accountant position. We'd like to have it both ways. We want lots of cheap, well-rounded experts whose most dearly held lifetime goal is to line up behind us waiting to be told what to do to keep our clients happy. It always worked before. But the days of growing secretaries into audit partners are likely gone for good.

In those days, the Giants operated our firms a lot more like apprenticeships than professional development systems, but with feudal landlord overtones. The succession systems depended not so much on procedural expertise and the filling of a specific customer technical need, but more on one's position on the value-creation team. Loyalties to senior-partner patrons and junior charges were forged in the trenches as we worked together, completely dependent on one another to fill a specific role in the value-creation system that served them.

That value-creation system also served as the foundation for a laddering succession system. That is, doers of work followed great client servers who followed the best rainmakers. That process repeated itself as a new rainmaker carved new territory and his successor client-servers and doers-of-work followed him. So it was your *position* in the value-creation system that bound you together, not your technical expertise.

Because we needed one another to be successful, not surprisingly, we were profoundly committed to one another. Then, as now, it wasn't practitioner-to-practitioner commitment that led to great value-creation systems, but the other way around. That commitment was the *result* of our interdependency in the value-creation system. The lesson we can take here is that obtaining young CPA commitment isn't the first step we need to worry about in planning for succession. It will be a natural, even unavoidable, outcome of successfully creating and deploying our new value-creation systems.

The Extinction of the Finders

As you might think, the Finders in the Days of the Giants served an important and unique role. We know from experience that, as a rule, accountants are skeptical and fiscally conservative; our professional function historically demanded it. We mostly need to stand in critical judgment of the world around us. And we're less inclined to think of that world as a land of unlimited opportunity than we are to want to measure what happened in it yesterday and worry about whether the trend will continue tomorrow. So without enough Finders, our rainmakers, a firm didn't stand a chance of growing. The Finders we had were invaluable to us.

But then, in the 1990s, a strange thing started happening. As unit-of-output productivity began dramatically increasing with the introduction of decentralized computing power, our CPAs began getting expensive. They eventually became so expensive that our Finders were less able to promise, "Anything you want at a price you can afford." Now, it was, "Anything you want, but at a price I have to charge." Price pressure began accelerating with the continuing advance of the computer microchip, and the Minders and Grinders began to get *really expensive*.

On top of price pressure, the velocity of rulemaking and other aspects of our bodies of professional knowledge began accelerating with the global communication capability of the Internet. It was now fast and easy to change tax rates, issue new accounting standards, devise more complex financial instruments, and monitor and operate in international markets. Whatever geo-socio-econo-politico whim our society had could quickly be turned into the law of the land, elaborated upon, and disseminated worldwide. The critical details that you simply had to know to stay current in your specialty were multiplying exponentially.

So specialization began to take a further toll on our Finders. "Anything you want, but at a price I have to charge" became, "Let me check back at the firm, and see if we have anyone that does that kind of work." It was a painful time for the Finders. Having come full circle from the glory days of "If you have the work you can get the people" to the far narrower world of "If you have the people you can get the work" was too much for our Finders. We began losing them, for the most part, in the mid-1990s and replacing them with the more efficient salespeople.

What we lost as a profession at that time is most importantly recognized for what we lost in terms of our value-creation capabilities. *We lost the ability to continually expand our deliverables.* It was the first important blow to our ability to create value, but not the last. Now, when our salespeople walked into a room, unlike our "anything and everything" Finders, they were looking for very specific needs reflected in our now-reduced set of deliverables. The message from management was, "Sell what we know how to do." It certainly seemed the quickest way to achieve the revenue growth we enjoyed in the days of the Finders.

Unfortunately, those salespeople now arrived at client offices not to solve client problems, but to sell specialist procedures. As one of my clients used to say, "Accounting firms now arrive not to provide me with what I need, but to sell me what they have." I couldn't think of a more damning—and accurate—statement on the condition of value creation in our firms.

My client's story was my first hint at what it might take to build and run a value-creation system of the future. Process engineers talk about everything in terms of inputs, processes, and outputs. Our Finders were constantly putting upward pressure on output variability by selling anything and everything. And in the Days of the Giants, we could do more things more easily, providing build-to-suit solutions in our low-input-variability world, the one of our cheap, generally skilled Grinders. As our Grinders got more specialized, it put predictable downward pressure on our ability to create value by serving unique customer wants at an acceptable market price.

But it's important to note that the loss of the Finders was clearly not about differing generational values or the personal commitment of CPA practitioners to one another. It was about functional irrelevance. Like the dinosaurs, the Finders died the death of any creature that cannot adapt to its environment. That's not to say that their loss wasn't an important one. It was. And that loss happened at the edge of the same cliff over which the Minders would inevitably tumble.

The Minders Follow the Finders

For our Minders, the sky was still the limit. For the time being, they had enough cheap, generally skilled labor to create value without worrying too much about the efficiency of the processes that intervened between labor inputs and client outputs. We had paper, spreadsheets, good ideas, and cheap labor. We could still solve a lot of the world's ills despite the dwindling numbers of Finders. But then two important things happened.

Enron and WorldCom

The corporate malfeasance laid bare during the days of Enron and WorldCom caused a sudden, massive resource reallocation via the federal legislation known as the Sarbanes–Oxley (SOX) Act of 2002. That sudden, permanent funding shift pushed accounting resources away from our traditional role as opinion givers on periodic financial information. More of those resources now went to the critical societal need for transparency and real-time information that was not being provided by our traditional function. For those of us who could provide SOX-related services, profits were immediate and significant. It almost had the feel of the heyday of financial statement auditing. Profits were plentiful because of the sudden labor leverage provided by the SOX legislation. But at the same time, seeds were being sown for lower profits in our traditional core services, because SOX-related profits were being drawn from old service areas. And talk of our services becoming commodities intensified.

The Great Recession

The second event leading to the demise of our Minder Giants was the Great Recession itself. To increase profits, firms looked to the one place they historically could—chargeable time. Minders in the value-creation systems of the Giants generally performed less procedural than "relationship" work, which involved monitoring customer perception of value and the retooling of processes to maximize that perception.

Minders gave up billable time to the producers of most of that work—the Grinders—to nurture their enthusiastic participation, goodwill, and loyalty in value-creation pursuits. Bluntly put, it was considered bad leadership form for Minders to insist on charging their time in preference to the folks carrying water for them.

So we're now poised to begin losing those "relationship" partners, or our Minders. And with that necessary loss will come the loss of personal commitment to *horizontal integration of our now-shrinking set of deliverables.* Our combined inability to expand deliverables and integrate the remaining ones will be devastating to our ability to realize much more in fees than the combined intrinsic, or commodity, value of everything we produce. And that will come nowhere near the business leverage requirements we've set for ourselves.

So the fate of the Minder dinosaurs is no less preordained than that of our Finder dinosaurs, but not because a retiring generation doesn't understand the needs of the next one. The loss of our Finders and Minders is due to simple inefficiency. That is, we can no longer afford to have expensive Finders sniffing around every corner for new deliverables that we don't have the expertise to produce. And we can no longer afford to have Minders spend time trying to figure out unique and creative ways to meet every consumer whim with increasingly specialized—and thus increasingly inflexible and expensive—human capital.

And, Last, the Grinders

Our Grinders, too, are falling victim to specialization demands. The two primary specialist avenues of audit and tax have long since given way to more vertical differentiation by industry, function, and region, for example. A young CPA that I interviewed said she'd started in our profession eight years ago, gradually progressing from general tax and audit work to providing income tax expertise in construction and real estate. Now, her focus has so narrowed that when a relative at a family get-together asked what her job involved, she quipped, "taxes for shopping centers."

So our Grinders were no less marginalized by the specialization demands of the marketplace than the Finders and Minders. Gone were the days when the simple willingness to work 3,000 hours a year while only reporting 2,300 would get you a seat at the table of the Giants. And now the generalist

Grinders are lining up behind the Minders to follow them out the door. And very soon.

Opportunity and Security Diverge

When thought of in terms of lean process engineering, what the Giant Finder, Minder, and Grinder teams were able to achieve together was to continually expand deliverables—as well as their value—through horizontal integration. But despite the inefficiency in our value-creation capabilities back then, we never heard talk of our products and services having become "commodities." That came later as our Finders, Minders, and Grinders began to fade from view.

The loss of our old succession system is at the core of our value-creation and commitment crises not because we discarded the Finder, Minder, and Grinder functions. It's because we haven't come up with a rational plan to replace that system. We're now facing firms filled mostly with specialists, each knowing how to produce their special product. Those products will each have vertically constructed linear production systems, none of which will intersect with any other of a firm's specialist offerings for "efficiency" reasons.

This constriction of our remaining deliverables and their horizontal integration is at the core of our value-creation and commitment crisis. And it's a downward spiral, one from which we won't recover until we deal with its root causes.

Today we have salespeople selling a reduced set of deliverables for our specialist producers. The removal of the final vestiges of practitioner-led value creation that so effectively bound our Giants together has now been largely accomplished. Today our highly skilled specialist producers aren't connected to a *system of creating value,* but to their *colleagues in the same department* who share a common view of the world around them. So specialization—while brought about by market demand—has reduced practitioners' relevance to one another.*

As an illustration of the disconnect among departments, I recall talking with a colleague about junior staff development and how we should use new hires. Should we use them broadly among departments before allowing them to specialize? Or should we assign them to a department from the

---

* The sheer hubris it took for us to seriously discuss increasing practitioners' commitment while at the same time discouraging their relevance to one another is pretty striking, if you think about it.

outset so they'd more quickly become productive in our highly demanding specialties? There wasn't any real question in my mind that we should lengthen their professional training period. By exposing them to as many different specialties as we could, I reasoned, we would not so drastically limit the breadth of experience of the top executives who would eventually replace us.

During our talk, I also asked that colleague about the culture of two specific departments and their connection to one another. Specifically, I asked him if there were any points of intersection between the two departments, so that I might start moving them together to try to expand the horizontal development of the junior accountants. I'd opened the discussion by saying that there didn't seem to be much interaction among CPA personnel in the two departments, and he said, "They could be in separate buildings."

While I wasn't really shocked by his answer, it didn't occur to me right then that we'd lost one important form of interdependency and loyalty that kept our CPAs committed to one another, a commitment that was critical in the old value-creation system. That commitment had now shifted to their specific departments.

And the repercussions of that shift are significant. In the Finder, Minder, and Grinder value-creation system, young professionals looked up the ladder and saw *opportunity*. There were diverse opportunities for growth. New things. They were needed by their firms' value-creation teammates and by many clients for many things. But perhaps just as important, looking up that ladder they saw *security*. The belief that we're critically needed by others in pursuit of a "holy mission" reduces the natural fear we all have of being abandoned. In the Days of the Giants, there was a solid *marriage* of opportunity and security. Both could be pursued with the same choice. Grow with the firm and its clients.

But today, when young professionals look up the ladder, they see one or maybe two positions to aspire to as ultimate career goals. Clients now need young CPAs not to accomplish a group goal, but to fill a specific technical function. Now, fear of abandonment is held at bay by departmental loyalties rather than clients and value-creation teammates. In this new specialist world, the lure of opportunity is *divorced* from the comfort of security. Junior CPAs now have to choose one or the other: the *security* of departmental loyalties—where opportunities are severely constricted—or *opportunity*, which now lies in the mission-based world of value creation *outside your firms in industry.*

And those opportunities are growing fast. Employment statistics prior to 2002 showed the employment growth curves in public and private accounting to be substantially identical in terms of percentages. The sudden rise of accountants in private industry around that time was understandably attributed to the SOX legislation. That decoupling of growth rates subsided momentarily around the time of the Great Recession, and as such it was easy to believe that the SOX growth curve was a temporary blip on the radar screen.

But now it's clear that the growth rate in private industry employment has begun eclipsing that of ours in public accounting again, with no relief in sight. The new mission—now driven by engagement, transparency, relevance, and stakeholder choices—is eclipsing our own self-defined one of independence and opinion on financial information. And the growing demand for private industry accountants has already begun to drive up the cost of our CPA inputs without a corresponding ability to charge more for what we do.

Unfortunately, most of our CPA delivery system guns are trained on a battlefield that's being rapidly abandoned by everyone else. And where those departing combatants are going should give us very good information on what our new value-creation systems might look like and how our practitioners will function together in them.

For example, over lunch one day, a friend who worked at a publicly held company described how the traditional accounting function of periodic earnings and financial position had shrunk so dramatically in the last couple of years. In the same breath, he noted there was correspondingly rapid and substantial growth in accounting personnel assigned to what they now referred to as "decision support."

It's this new mission of addressing societal demand for decision-making material and real-time transparency of timely, relevant information that will continue to shrink the specialist pie for folks still lingering around the watering hole of year-end process. And it will be the driving force in determining demand for new CPAs whether we decide to join that mission or not.

The Clinical Analogy

To show how restoring practitioner-led value creation is critical to engage junior practitioners, I needed a sound analogy—preferably one in a profession under even greater pressure to use specialists in more valuable ways.

And I found that analogy in medicine, which has taken the same professional journey we have but is much farther along the path of needing to provide more valuable outcomes with an increasingly specialized and isolated practitioner population.

The Mayo brothers, Charles and William, were the first to recognize early in the twentieth century that medical specialization had led consumers to believe that quality of medical care was *declining* as a result. That belief persists today, despite our living almost twice as long as we did a hundred years ago. It persists despite the fact that diseases formerly thought of as automatic death sentences have now become management problems.

But the Mayo brothers wisely chose not to dismiss public perception of quality of care. Specialization in medicine, although necessary, had led to a fragmentation of services that did not serve patients well. So the Mayos sought to create a clinical system that would reconnect those services for the good of the patient. They believed they could achieve superior health outcomes using an holistic approach that emphasized teamwork, respect, preventive care, specialty integration, and patient involvement. So they assigned each patient one physician who'd be responsible for that patient's entire journey through the clinical system. As Dr. William Mayo* explained in the early part of the twentieth century:

> It has become necessary to develop medicine as a cooperative science; the clinician, the specialist and the laboratory workers uniting for the good of the patient. Individualism in medicine can no longer exist.

The Days of the Giants were numbered at the Mayo Clinic from that day forward. But disillusionment can often set in after years of practice, as Dr. Ofri mentions in *Why Would Anyone Choose to Become a Doctor?* What started out as a noble desire to cure the sick can give way to the feeling that government and business bureaucracies have dampened their sense of mission. *But their initial idealistic expectation is mission-based.* That is, they sign on to accomplish something important; otherwise they never would have made the commitment to become a doctor in the first place.

As I look at our young charges in the profession and see their specialization-induced isolation, it's hard to imagine how—without a value-creation mission as compelling as medicine's "cure the sick"—we can even dream

---

* Mayo, William James. Commencement address, Rush Medical College, Chicago, 1910.

that many of them would make the commitment to remain. Our junior specialist practitioners get to suffer all the disillusionment with none of the mission-fueled motivation to get them through the trying times of too much work and too little accomplishment.

That is the critical challenge of building practitioner-led value creation in our own profession, and we'd be wise to keep it in mind as we plan for our own growth and relevance. The marketplace isn't going to wake up one morning and tell us we're wonderful and that it's satisfied with our performance. We need a goal no less compelling and simple than that of medicine's as we ask our junior colleagues to join us and commit to one another in pursuit of it. It will be the cornerstone of practitioner-led value creation. And it will be the glue necessary to support anything like the owner-equity systems that we enjoy today.

As in the medical profession, the market's message to us will always be one of demanding greater value. And as we in accounting struggle to meet that demand, we can again look to the medical profession for inspiration on how to begin. In an April 2011 presentation of the MPR News *Bright Ideas* series on Minnesota Public Radio, Dr. Nicholas LaRusso, director of the Mayo Clinic's Center for Innovation, spoke of a simple mission statement for the medical profession. He said that medicine should provide *more services* to *more people, more valuably,* and at a *declining cost.*

So in the new, harsher world of the accounting profession, we would be wise to emulate that mission. And we'll need a goal no less compelling— and simple—than that of medicine's "cure the sick." Without it, we'll be too easily defeated by the marketplace as our increasingly isolated junior specialist CPAs spend more and more of their time deciding when it's time to bolt to the mission-based "decision support" function in industry.

The accounting profession is at that point in our history where we need to make the same choice that the Mayo brothers made so long ago. It's the first of the three important market commitments we'll need to make to lay the foundation for building the value-creation systems that will rebuild mission-fueled practitioner commitment to one another. Just as the Mayo brothers did nearly a century ago, we must now commit to building value-creation systems that will be led by our practitioners.

Chapter 3

Clash of the Titans

There's a book about the future of professional firms that I admire: *The Firm of the Future,* by Paul Dunn and Ron Baker.* In it, they make the following statement:

> Yet the debate between the generalist and specialist is over, and the latter has won. The accounting profession is one of the last professions to have specialized; doctors started in the 1940s, lawyers in the 1950s.

This simple statement neatly defines a constraint in our firms' developmental capabilities. It's critical that we continue the path toward the market's demand for specialization. More expertise is a good thing.

Unfortunately, though—good convergent problem-solving experts that we are—our tendency is to want to lower the number of variables in our equations to more reliably execute their algorithms. So when we think about the demand from the marketplace to specialize, we slide easily into unrestrained spending, pursuing that as if no other constraint competed with it. Specialist expertise becomes good, and anything in its path becomes evil.

But the ability to think about your firm's development—the real daily decisions about who to train for what and how to devise production systems—is not that simple. That is, we can't simply identify the constraints and then attack each one separately by engaging in a linear, convergent problem-solving equation with only one variable. Intuitively, we all know that life

---

* Dunn, Paul, and Ronald J. Baker. *The Firm of the Future: A Guide for Accountants, Lawyers, and Other Professional Services.* Hoboken, NJ: John Wiley & Sons, 2003.

is much more complex than that: Many constraints compete with each other. And that ambiguity does not make for a fun planning environment.

But in developing your firm, the exercise of identifying the market constraints competing with one another, and then planning for all of them simultaneously, is a critical one. If you don't, you run the risk of treating each constraint separately and not viewing your firm's value-delivery capabilities as one integral constraints-management system that requires optimization to operate at peak performance.

The overwhelmingly universal human response to information that life gives us every day is to immediately filter it down to things that confirm our own values. We're no different from anyone else in that tendency. So when we hear "specialize," we hear that as a call to refine our inputs to the exclusion of everything else. It's what we do, and we're good at it. The market *demands* it from us.

But what we don't hear as clearly from the marketplace is, "Specialize, but only within the constraint of our willingness to pay you." This is our cue to throw up our hands, roll our eyes, and ask, "Well, which is it? Greater specialist expertise or unlimited outcomes? We have to know so we can move in the right direction."

The vexing answer, of course, is both. Up until now, our overwhelming response to the call to specialize has been to refine our inputs and limit them to the procedural elements needed to produce lots of outputs at a uniform level of (very high) procedural quality. Then, we sit back at management team meetings and scratch our heads. How did it come to be that our services have become commodities? And why don't our clients value us the way they used to?

Conversely, if we would have chosen the other "winner" in the war between specialization and the market's demand for valuable outcomes, as our remaining Minder Giants might like, we'd be submitting to the customer's desire for unlimited variable outcomes by spending unlimited specialist resources in pursuit of them. But in doing so, we'd fall out of the market's tolerance for paying us just as surely as if we'd responded solely to the pressure to specialize.

Flavor of the Month

In an environment where competing constraints are not recognized and treated as parts of a cohesive, whole plan, there's a crippling side effect. A certain cynicism and demotivation occurs when each new initiative doesn't yield the solution it promised. Senior partners refer to this as a flavor-of-the-month approach to firm development and use it as an easy way to ignore change with a this-too-shall-pass attitude. Initiatives can be cynically dismissed by naysayers because "they told you so" when competing forces naturally push in another direction.

A quick example of this is in staff development. Specialization is an important constraint, as we all know from Dunn and Baker and our daily lives. That tells us to limit educational breadth and development of our junior practitioners as quickly as possible to achieve the specialization the market demands. Our paperless process initiatives are the "room" designed to isolate our practitioners from one another and create specialists as quickly as possible.

But the marketplace also tells us that breadth of experience teaches practitioners to understand their specialist roles in a wider context. The delivery of outcomes depends on specialists having a wider view than only their procedural contributions, so we're encouraged to lengthen their development at the same time we're asked to shorten it. The human-capital function champions these types of initiatives, and they have their own special "room" at the firm for their activities.

Now introduce a third constraint. Competition in the marketplace for our human capital—and the very specialization we're trying to respond to by shortening the developmental path of our professionals—is creating more diverse opportunities for them. Career specialization at a very young age can be a relatively permanent, and potentially limiting, career decision. So any firm's internal program that intends to lengthen the developmental period of young practitioners can easily be attacked analytically as working against specialization.

It's this lurching from constraint to constraint that leads our firms to spend enormous amounts of time and money, causes paralyzing partner cynicism, and demotivates everyone involved. Each time one of those programs is launched, there are presumed winners and losers, and they're kept, for the most part, in separate developmental rooms to eliminate conflict.

In our case here, the human-capital function is energized by a widening scope of training and having a great time spending its allotment of investment funds in the process. The fans of specialization, not necessarily in agreement with that investment philosophy, are nevertheless having their own field day refining their linear process environments to promote specialization. It should not be surprising that our nearly extinct Minder Giants see both of these developmental efforts as not contributing to their ability to turn the car keys over to their successors.

The market reality is that all three of those constraints are important and unrelenting deciders of junior practitioner development. If your firm responds to this competition by creating an environment where people of different perspectives get to go off in their respective corners to commiserate with people who share their own values, your firm's development will be slow and costly. And you will not easily and profitably get to the Days of the New Giants.

Accounting firm development doesn't have to be a flavor-of-the-month, win-lose, zigzagging proposition. Constraints management can lead to conflict. It *should* lead to conflict because engaging in a process to combine the values and capabilities of all of your specialist practitioners into a value-creation machine will involve a cost-efficient, adaptive response to the natural competition of conflicting market demands.

The uncomfortable truth about what we face today as our Minders and Grinders leave the building is that the specialists we leave behind have no choice but to deal with the value-creation deficit in our firms in a fundamentally different way than we did. And it's not because we come from different generational perspectives, but because we're no longer cheap enough and generally skilled enough to *simultaneously provide unlimited variable outcomes to our clients and define quality on our own terms*, like we did in the Days of the Giants. The marketplace wants outcomes, and yet we still insist on defining practice quality through our own values first before we consider giving the economy what it wants.

This is a really hard message for a profession whose stock in trade has always been founded in the giving of opinions on things. We still actually get paid to opine, so it's very hard not to look at the world and want to retain our ability to end all conversations with our professional opinion about something. The notion of needing to balance our specialist offerings with the market's demand for value can leave a bad taste in our mouths. It's the professional equivalent of having to ask, "Do you want fries with that?" in the course of our service delivery.

I'll Be the Judge of That!

For us to come up with a different opinion about the market balance between specialization and consumer-defined outcomes, it might help if we were to take on the role of *consumer* of professional services instead of the *provider* of them. We can then give our opinion about constraints management as a helpful concept.

As providers, we tell ourselves and prospective clients that we have the best tax, accounting, and audit professionals in our market, and we bring a unique value to customers that they can't get anywhere else. We're obligated to make that statement and, for the most part, actually believe it.

But think for a moment about the thought process you might undergo when purchasing surgical services for yourself or a loved one, for example. You might have a referral from your primary-care physician, or you might have been sent to a clinical provider simply as a matter of being in the same health-care system as the referring specialist physician. Maybe a friend or neighbor has had an experience recently with that specialist.

Whatever the case, when you think about it, it's painfully obvious that we have no way to reliably evaluate a surgeon's competence by predicting which one will provide the most expert and highly skilled services. The truth is, when hiring specialist medical services, those services are *entirely and appropriately* valued purely by supply and demand at a presumed uniform level of competence. That sounds like a pretty good working definition of a commodity!

So the depressing reality is that your clients are no more capable of valuing your services any more highly than their procedural (or commodity) cost, similar to the situation with our medical counterparts. They're not equipped to assess your skills and have no way of predicting in advance an overall outcome that would include your performance as a specialist.

The one thing they can learn to expect, though, in the course of working inside of a well-designed and operated clinical system, is the likelihood of a positive outcome. That's because outcomes are *human experiences*. In other words, how a client feels after interaction with you and your firm defines "how good" a practitioner you are in his eyes, just like our good surgeon above. To illustrate this, witness a recent interaction I had with the medical profession.

Me and My Knee

Thirty years ago, I needed to have a rather large piece of cartilage surgically removed from my knee. I remember asking the surgeon if there might be implications for that loss of buffering tissue someday when I was old, like, 60 or something. He looked at me sort of curiously and said, "Well, of course." I was young enough to still have the childlike expectation that any doctor's first job was to reassure me that "this too shall pass," and it was the first time a medical professional didn't do that for me. So I knew that someday another surgical joint intervention of some kind might be necessary.

Fast forward to a couple of years ago around the winter holidays. My surgically altered knee began to hurt something terrible, and I was hobbling along just barely able to get to the office and uncomfortably do my job. The meeting with my family physician went as you might expect it. She reminded me that carrying the extra twenty-five pounds I'd gained since quitting smoking probably wasn't helping things. But she referred me to a surgeon in their clinical system to evaluate me for a possible knee replacement.

My meeting with the surgeon indicated that my knee was indeed in bad shape. But, he offered, the relative amount of pain people have in similar cases varies widely. There was the possibility that injections might temporarily relieve the pain and delay the inevitable joint replacement. Since I've always thought that original, factory-installed equipment is best whenever possible, I agreed to the injections.

As the days turned into weeks, it became apparent that other joints in my body were hurting, too. In particular, my shoulders became so sensitive to movement that I was unable to move my elbows away from my body. A simple handshake was excruciatingly painful as my fingers became inflamed. Then came an encounter at what I believed would be my final presurgical meeting with my knee replacement surgeon.

As I described my other joint issues, he shrugged. It was outside of what he was concerned about. All he was focused on was my knee replacement surgery. He used the latest in computer-assisted techniques, he assured me. He'd performed hundreds of similar procedures over the course of his career. I should have every confidence in the quality of the procedure. Although I'd pretty much accepted that my knee needed replacing at that point, I began to pressure him on the other symptoms. Were the other joint problems normal? What the heck was going on with me?

As a departing aside, just as he was stepping out of the room, he asked, "Have you seen a rheumatologist?" He wasn't going to refer me to one. That would be the job of my family doctor, but he was just curious and thought maybe doing so would make sense.

So I made another appointment with my family doc. She ran a battery of tests intended to diagnose rheumatoid arthritis. Although all of the indicators proved negative, she referred me to a rheumatologist based on a single test result that indicated inflammation generally.

It was time to enter the practice world of yet another specialist who didn't view it as his job to coordinate a bunch of murky diagnostic information. His job was to diagnose rheumatoid arthritis and treat it within prescribed rheumatology specialist practice methodology, which he did quickly and efficiently. I was to begin taking a drug to control the inflammation and reduce the presumed joint damage that should begin occurring if I left the condition untreated.

The side effects of this drug were potentially nasty. In fact, they could be life threatening in some cases. I was assured that the toxicity was just something to monitor over time to see how well I tolerated it. Intuitively, I was set to rebel. I didn't really feel *that* bad, because the overall inflammation condition had been subsiding slightly. In fact, the combination of gradually receding overall joint pain and the disappearance of it in my knee via injection had me thinking that I really didn't want to start taking a drug that could kill me. As the dutiful and obedient patient that we were all taught to be, though, I filled the prescription.

The pill bottle sat on the kitchen counter for a few days before I decided to address it. I picked it up and reread the potential side effects. I reevaluated my overall health. Sure, I was over fifty now. My blood sugar was too high. My cholesterol levels were approaching the upper end of reference levels. All of my friends and acquaintances seemed to be complaining of the same things. I decided that I really didn't hurt enough to jeopardize my immune system with the prescribed drug, and my knee didn't hurt badly enough to make me replace it. So I threw the meds out and resolved to wait and see.

But the entire set of encounters with the medical professionals had set the wheels in motion for change. As we age, it becomes frighteningly apparent that we don't really get to control much of anything about the future. So when I began to think harder about my health, it seemed like a wise course of action to consider controlling the things I *could* control.

At this point, I was now forty to fifty pounds overweight. My twenty-five pounds of smoking-cessation weight had been added to fifteen pounds of middle-age spread. Another ten pounds came with the temporary steroid prescription during my rheumatoid evaluation. It certainly couldn't hurt my knees and hips to lose that weight, so I set about doing so. Not only that, I fundamentally changed how I approached food and began to get a good handle on eating for the right reasons. My family-practice physician had recommended as much several years ago.

In addition to that, I went for treatment and evaluation at a spinal care clinic specializing in weight training for the musculature of the back. Within a year I'd transformed what was becoming chronic daily pain into a completely resolved situation. Imagine! Diet and exercise! Who knew?

As it turns out, my primary-care physician knew. In addition to the structural changes in my daily regimen that may have delayed or eliminated a lifetime need for joint replacements and invasive treatment of my aching back, I'd significantly lowered my risk factors for heart disease and diabetes as well.

When I think of the outcome, or the human experience, of that two-year journey, I credit the clinical system for the delivery of the overall experience. Most important, I found that the value of my experience was not contained inside the procedural expertise of those practitioners. Rather, the value was in the *ultimate positive outcome* I'd experienced. It was in how I *felt* about the overall result.

As with any well-designed and -executed outcome-producing system, one of the hallmarks was the presence of an actively engaged patient, me, making health-care decisions in full knowledge of the interplay among all of the body's systems and their relative individual conditions as described to me by my family physician. It struck me that she was the integrator, my Minder, of all procedural expertise and the clearinghouse of all relevant information that helped guide my decision making toward the best outcome. I was a very happy clinical buyer.

Her own decision making, on the other hand, was limited to applying decision trees, or medical-practice algorithms, to my symptoms that were based in sound medical evidence. Condition A that presents with symptom B indicates Test C, and so forth. *The important decisions were left to me.*

My experience with the medical profession left me thinking that, in the case of my own profession, we might need to start trying to increase the value of our specialist offerings by tinkering less with our expert procedural processes and more with the decisions and advice that surround those procedures. We might then be able to effectively address the market demand that we produce outcome-based results. But to get our business leverage moving back in the right direction, we'd need to get the ratio of the competing market constraints of specialist expertise and valuable outcomes more in balance.

At the start of our journey in Chapter 1, we learned about the important market commitment firms must make to reestablish practitioner-led value creation. That reconnection of our practitioners via a joint commitment to the delivery of an expanding set of valuable outcomes will once again offer our young CPAs the diverse growth opportunities and the comfort of a secure future that they'll rightly expect from us as we grow our profession.

The Customer Is Always...Responsible

But we're still a couple of market commitments short of the cultural foundation we need to make a plan to resolve the combined value-creation and commitment crisis that make up the succession problem facing our profession. Happily, the next commitment your firm needs to make to begin to rebuild its value-creation capabilities is already paid for.

Your only barrier is to make the political decision to reallocate some production costs to achieve a better balance of the competing constraints of specialization and market value of our services. Still, it'll be a hard commitment to make, because it appears at first to strike at the very core of our professional values and important function as CPAs.

The next commitment your firm needs to make to begin digging itself out of the value-creation and commitment crisis is that your customer's perception of value must lead all of your process development efforts. When you think about it, it's perfectly logical. If we've outstripped our clients' willingness to pay for our specialization efforts and have accepted, as did the Mayo brothers nearly a century ago, that specialization was causing the perception of a *decline* in quality of care, then it makes perfect sense to get a handle on why that's occurring.

But the notion of adopting our client's perception of value in planning our production systems runs counter to all of the founding precepts of our original mission as accountants. The means of that mission were founded in remaining independent enough from our clients to render objective opinions. God forbid that a client's reaction to our services should influence how we deliver them in our future dealings. We'd lose our objectivity!

I can hear you saying, "Paul, this whole outcome-based practice world that you promote smacks of a world gone crazy—complete with client pandering, rampant conflict of interest, and an epidemic of illegal dealings. The client decides what's valuable to them, and we think first about providing that? Surely you're yanking our professional chains."

Of course, we know that at the height of the economic bubble around the turn of the last century that culminated with Enron and WorldCom, our professional formula for simultaneously providing client value and fulfilling our mission to the public via independent opinion giving was woefully inadequate. It did nothing to prevent the very client pandering, rampant conflict of interest, and epidemic of illegal dealings that we fear would be caused by adopting client value as a presumptive standard in the conduct of our work. We certainly can't do any worse a job than we did of seeing to the interests of third-party stakeholders by first listening to learn how our customers feel.

However, the process of aligning client, third-party stakeholder, and practitioner interests is an important precondition to the growth that your firm needs today. It's no secret that our own self-defined means of independence and opinion giving is losing ground to what technology and globalism are forcing upon us. And that new means-of-the-mission for protecting the public interest and third-party stakeholders simultaneously is contained now in relevance, transparency, and choices.

It shouldn't shock us any longer that the value of opinions of any kind—whether they're about earnings, financial position, the likelihood of future conditions continuing, or anything at all—are becoming severely limited by the dynamic nature of capital formation in the world today. Expert opinions take too much time to produce to maintain relevance to anyone's decision-making processes. It's no one's fault. It's simply the nature of opinions. By the time they're rendered, their relevance has usually passed or become measurably impaired.

So if all that parties-in-interest really want from us is transparency of all relevant information so that they can make better decisions, it should be an easy commitment to make. Everyone wants it. But there are important parts of human nature that work against us in easily and cost-efficiently delivering these things.

Client Choices: The Value of Doing Less

When clients come before us, just as we do when we go to our doctors, they have a way of projecting their needs that implies that they'd like us to simply make them "all better," much as children expect when they approach their parents. Very much like I wanted my knee surgeon of thirty years ago to merely reassure me, they want us to be Giants for them. Unfortunately, this customer phenomenon influences accounting practitioners to do two things that are devastating to their firms' value-creation capabilities.

First, at the initial sign of a client or stakeholder need, we tend to evaluate all possible outcomes regardless of their likelihood of occurring, just as our past Giants in medicine and accounting did. We don't present all of the information, but it's there in case we need it—a hideously expensive and not very valuable way to conduct professional practice. Resources are not unlimited as they were in the Days of the Giants.

Second, and perhaps more important, after that excessive analysis, we make recommendations based on *our* interpretation of customers' needs instead of presenting all relevant information for them to use to make *their own* risk-based decisions. By excluding our customers (or our children or medical patients) from using available relevant information to make their own decisions, we actually reduce the value of their clinical experience.

This important cost-shifting principle cannot be overemphasized. It turns out that an important part of the job of migrating toward the new means of our professional mission is to stop impairing the value of what we do by taking decision-making power away from our clients.

I was first introduced to this important concept of creating value by cost-shifting to the customer by watching Thomas Friedman give a speech on television about the airlines' value-creation maneuver of having turned us all into our own enthusiastic ticketing agents. We happily compete with one another for preferred seating and pricing through online services. In short, the airlines have turned us into their employees, and we're happily paying them for the privilege. It's a tidy little example of how service providers can provide far more value by making all relevant information instantly available along with an array of available choices rather than indulging in the higher-contact, more-expensive, and considerably less-valuable way of doing it for them.

In my medical journey, I'd been projecting to my medical service providers that I wanted them to make me "all better" and to reassure me about the future. Despite how I presented myself, the most valuable thing they did for me was not to respond to me by overexpending valuable resources on far-flung clinical analysis of anything and everything that might come into play in my health care. They're under significant market pressure to simply get all relevant information in front of me so that I can make my own decisions about what it would take to increase the likelihood of a positive overall result.

On to Commitment Number Three

Now you have two of the three critical marketplace commitments in place that you'll need to begin to reconstruct your value-creation systems. The first commitment to rejoin your CPAs into a practice system rooted in value creation is essential to regaining the powerful glue that will make CPA practice a team sport again. Practitioners must lead value delivery at the clinic, or all we'll be doing in the future is vending specialist procedures at commodity prices.

The second commitment of deciding to place the customer's perception of value *first* in the consideration of all firm-development efforts will start us back on the path to balancing the competing constraints of specialization and outcome-based market value. As much as we might like to return to the Days of the Giants, we need to accept that they're over for good.

But the final commitment you must make to complete the foundation for your firm's transformation into a value-creation engine is the most important. It will provide the missionary focus that will give your practitioners the energy and resolve to start building the value-creation ship they'll need very soon on the sea of their future practice world.

However, for them to gather the collective will to build that ship, they'll first need to feel *absolutely compelled* to go to the place where the winds are already blowing them. If we first try to "drum up the men to gather wood, divide the work and give orders"* without proper leadership, they'll begin this important work as reluctant slave labor who fear and resent their masters instead of the missionary seekers of the future gathered at the front of the ship, ready to face the monsters and dragons on a hazy horizon.

If we want our practitioners to build that value-creation ship, we must first "teach them to yearn for the vast and endless sea."† With this last commitment, and its marriage of value creation to the new tools of the mission of accountancy, they'll not only gather the will to build it, but they'll do so happily and with missionary purpose.

---

* De Saint-Exupéry, Antoine. *The Wisdom of the Sands*. New York: Harcourt, Brace and Co., 1950.
† Ibid.

Chapter 4

Creating Missionary Resolve

When I think of the term *value creation*, I think of an empty vessel. Certainly, the consuming public wants valuable stuff. To the extent that any of us learns what customers value and then finds a way to produce it in a way that makes them willing to pay more than its commodity cost, we've created value and, by association, profitability.

But we know that truly great companies don't just cast about randomly looking for ways to make money simply for the sake of making money. That's why they have mission statements. Value creation needs a preferred social context to bind producers to consumers of that value. Our connection as buyers and sellers needs to be about more than making money and spending it. To gain the enthusiastic participation, or traction, between producers and consumers, each transaction needs to be about something more exalted than "Let's make as much money as we possibly can."

So consumption cannot be the goal, but only a means to achieving one. Look at no less of a consumption-oriented company than Walmart, for example. The company's original mission statement was "to give ordinary folk the chance to buy the same things as rich people." Over time, it became the somewhat more sanitized version, "Save money. Live better," but it's fundamentally Sam Walton's original statement minus the economic class overtones.

We clearly need a battleground to which we can send our newly constructed value-creation teams to inspire their efforts with the sense of mission that will keep them engaged not only with one another as value-creation teammates, but with their customers in pursuit of a great purpose. This is the final foundational commitment your firm needs to make to address the concerns of the Giants. It won't be easy, but it's critical to your future growth.

Lots to Do, Little to Accomplish

A human-capital specialist working in my firm unwittingly described to me the depth of the disconnect of CPA practitioners from their work environments that has evolved over the last quarter century. During our conversation about young CPAs and their career thought processes, she said that they spent most of their time "deciding when it was time to go to the other side." That's not a shocking statement in and of itself. Our traditional role as auditors and givers-of-independent-opinion naturally would put us in an adversarial role that could lead to conflict with our customers. The idea that one might want to move from one mission to another would just be swapping one equally compelling mission for another.

But she clarified her statement further as I pressed her. No, it wasn't about *swapping* missions but about *getting* one. Young auditors no longer saw the opportunity we did in the Days of the Giants. Our audits and tax returns were no longer a stepping-stone to a wider value-creation universe. They were a never-ending specialist treadmill with little more purpose than to produce as many procedures as possible with fewer and fewer CPAs.

What those young professionals yearned for was to join a team that was pursuing a definable group goal, a purpose more compelling than getting more jobs done than last year with fewer people. And they saw their best chance of finding those teams as being in industry, not in public accounting.

As an indication of this troubling trend, the *Inside Public Accounting (IPA)* "2011 National Benchmarking Report"* states that two-thirds of its respondents had voluntary turnover that was greater than their involuntary terminations. The average ratio in all responding firms of voluntary departures compared to involuntary ones was 1.75 to 1.00. On average, seven employees leave for every four who are asked to do so.

Such a rate of voluntary departure in a recessionary environment paints a scary picture about what that scenario might look like as the business cycle improves. In view of that likelihood, the *IPA* editorial opinion about "giving employees something bigger within your firm to believe in"† seems understated.

* Platt Group. "National Benchmarking Report." *Inside Public Accounting,* 2011.
† Ibid.

Now I was starting to understand better what my young colleagues were thinking when they left. I recall asking a talented young man in our office about his choice of a tax department assignment instead of one on an audit team. His demonstrated skills development indicated a clear preference for information systems, and his technology skills very much suggested a promising career in auditing.

When I asked him about his choice, he said that when he went to do audits, he didn't always "feel welcome" by the client's staff. I dismissed his comment as that of a young person taking offhand comments too personally and that his skills development would eventually get him redirected to his best area of demonstrated skill.

But it was not to be. Don't get me wrong. This kid was bright enough to pick his intellectual ticket. It wasn't that he lagged in the tax department, but that his obvious analytical skills suggested another career path. It wasn't until later that I realized what he was actually saying to me.

It wasn't social pain associated with rejection that turned him off to working in one of our specialist auditor departments. It was the *reason* that the clients' staffs didn't make him "feel welcome." It wasn't that he was not a nice person or that they didn't like the fact that his work was potentially adversarial to their own, but that *his work was irrelevant to them.* They were busy working with current—and thus relevant—information, while it was his job to inquire about last year's information. They had long since cast most of that information out of their minds as not having much to do with anything meaningful to them.

Wow. Imagine working in a place where your relevance to your colleagues back at the firm is steadily shrinking because of specialization *and* your relevance to your clients' staff is disappearing because of allocative efficiency. Those two shrinking motivational connections are hardwired into the immediate future by two important, unrelenting constraints. Not only will they not improve in the near future; they will get much worse and much more quickly than you might imagine. Rather than be amazed that this is true, we should be shocked that the exodus isn't much larger than it already has been.

So with this trend in mind, I suggest that—until your firm makes the third critical market commitment needed to create an idealistic future vision for group accomplishment—your foundation for growth will be limited to piling specialist mill on top of specialist mill, producing commodity services for an increasingly fee-sensitive client base with a permanently rotating professional staff. This does not paint a pretty picture for equity succession in the coming decade.

I don't presume to suggest a mission statement for your firm, because it can take many forms and be said many ways. But there's a fundamental component you'll need to express to provide for practitioner engagement beyond the promise of "doing more jobs with fewer people than last year." The foundation of that mission is told best in the following story.

The Disappearing Department

I met a while ago with the vice president of internal control at a publicly traded company. He told me that in recent years his department had gone from about six or seven members down to two. The Great Recession had put the squeeze on all of us to do more with less, and his department was no exception.

However, there was an interesting twist to his dilemma. Originally, his staff of auditors reported directly to him. The object of such labor leverage is, of course, not only to accomplish the daily mission of protecting the company's assets and mitigating risk, but to provide for his own succession. In other words, the continuation of his department and the conduct of its value-creation capabilities were mutually assured in this arrangement. One of those staff members could bubble up in the natural course of business and eventually take over his role.

But a strange thing happened during the Great Recession. Not only was his staff size reduced to two auditors, but they no longer reported directly to him. The company had decided that young managerial talent would be deployed in his department for short tours of duty in a greater plan to develop diversely trained executive talent. The wider company need for managerial development had dictated that he not only make do with fewer resources, but that the company's continuation needs trumped those of his department. He was now effectively a "department of one" and had become one of the single-point-of-failure process-engineering risks he was responsible for avoiding.

It got even more interesting in a later meeting, when we had a more direct discussion about his company's overall business-continuation risks. His plan was to hire a national accounting firm to devise the basics of a continuation plan for the company because they had that expertise. He then planned to hire an internal full-time position at the company to maintain that continuation plan going forward. The strategy of purchasing expertise and then internalizing it was historically very solid. But something about it nagged at me.

Wouldn't that strategy actually increase continuation risk by having it maintained by a new hire, one who would be a "department of one" at the company? Wouldn't it make more sense to outsource not only the creation of the company's continuation plan, but to also outsource its implementation and maintenance over time from that same firm? That way, his department's contribution to value creation could be better maintained, or continued, than if the company waited for that executive to leave and then started all over each time there was turnover at that position.

A national accounting firm is likely to have hundreds of auditors available at any given moment, whereas my friend's company was unlikely to be in that position. We can paint an even more compelling picture of the opportunity when we think of those hundreds of available auditors busying themselves deciding when it was "time to join the other side." *What if we could become the "other side"?*

And I had stumbled upon our mission.

It's more than ironic. It's scary. How can we solve a problem for our clients that we haven't successfully solved for ourselves? To solve business-continuation exposure in public accounting (our succession crisis), do we first have to learn how to solve business-continuation risks for our clients?

The Merger of Value Creation and Succession

There are lots of ways to try to word a mission statement, I suspect. But if we're to take a legitimate swing at Nick LaRusso's means of pursuing the professional mission of "providing more services to more people, more valuably, and at a declining cost," we'll need something very big. Despite the fact that the primary means of serving our mission is changing dramatically, it can't change the fact that we're serving the public.

To best serve our mission, we need to start now to:

■ Move resources away from the paralyzing, isolating prospect of always trying to remain independent enough to give objective opinions about periodic financial information
■ Move resources toward becoming engaged enough to provide transparency of relevant information *so that people can make their own choices*

And we'll need to do so using as little permanent labor as possible in order to respond effectively to the economy's competing constraints. This sudden merging of the economy's demand for increased value and nonlabor-dependent succession has created a defining moment in our profession. It is the moment that affords us the opportunity to make a sustaining contribution to filling that value-management void that is now growing in the global economy.

But to respond to that opportunity to help our clients design, build, and maintain their own value-creation infrastructures as the living, breathing, and relatively permanent systems they need to be, we'll have to provide well-coordinated process and labor systems designed to cope with a shrinking, impermanent, and specialized labor supply.

This is our problem today, but it's also our clients' problem tomorrow. We in public accounting are simply going to step over that business-continuation crisis line sooner than our counterparts inside our clients' offices, because we've historically had a far smaller population that served far fewer specialties.

It's Not *My* Problem!

As a tax partner of recent vintage, I initially felt a bit smug about being able to lay the world's ills at the feet of my auditor friends, if only for a moment. It was easy to absolve myself, because my work wasn't founded in opinions. In practice, I'd do my best to make sure the tax returns I signed were correct. I'd analyze past transactions to predict ahead of time what my clients' tax burden might be so that they could plan. I might even suggest a current course of action to influence that future tax burden.

But I didn't need to worry too much about giving third parties an opinion about a current or future tax burden for a specific client's tax matters. So the means of the mission really didn't affect me all that much. I didn't have that relevance problem that my stuffy old auditor Giant colleagues had.

Or did I?

I thought about Tom Friedman's airline ticketing agent example. You'll recall that the airlines had learned how to turn customers into enthusiastic, unpaid ticketing agents by providing them not only with current ticketing information, but also an array of available choices that they could make to influence their ticketing status. The airlines were providing current—and thus *relevant*—information in a *transparent* manner, available to anyone on the Internet. Customers could then *make their own best risk-based decisions.* My definition of value creation and professional mission were starting to sound like one and the same.

I had to admit to myself that in my practice days, my work was not always aimed at providing clients with daily indicators of tax status and an array of choices for them to use in making their own decisions. Even in my nonauditing world of taxes, I was subjecting clients to opinions about a previous transaction stream, and then projecting the effects of continuing it. I also avoided telling clients anything at all until I'd thoroughly analyzed all possible outcomes.

That work tended to be highly laborious and analytical. And I'd conducted it nearly 100 percent out of my clients' sight, so I could prevent them from making decisions without totally complete and accurate information. Gulp.

This whole value-creation thing was starting to look like a much more systemic practice issue to me than merely having an audit model that wasn't changing with modern times. Everything going on around me seemed aimed at depriving the customer of timely information and decision-making power and, therefore, value. And we were doing so in the interest of accuracy and completeness—two very laudable qualities, to be sure. But we were allowing those qualities to trump relevance in most of our processes, much to the consternation of our increasingly value-conscious customers.

As a CPA, I'd been trained to think that value creation and the fulfillment of our mission as accountants were, by definition, in opposition to one another. If I was pursuing my professional mission with honor and skill, I'd proceed cautiously with my work, taking great care to be sure it didn't run afoul of a third-party's needs with a potential adverse interest to my client. Whether it was the investing public, a current or potential banker, vendor, customer, or business partner, I had to be on my toes to make sure I'd positioned myself as the dispassionate judge in the room.

Now I was getting information that value creation and professional mission were actually coming into alignment. Our clients, their third-party stakeholders, and investors were all but screaming at me that they didn't really want or need a judge in the room any longer. All they wanted was timely, relevant information and an array of available choices to make. They were perfectly happy making their own decisions and taking risks that they knew perfectly well existed. They just wanted more relevant information to use in making those decisions.

But I certainly don't intend to suggest that we all abandon auditing as we know it. That's neither realistic nor desirable. But to move forward as a growing profession, our firms have to get a tight grip on how value creation is becoming irretrievably married to the pursuit of professional mission. Not only can they coexist with one another, but they're now intrinsically and permanently connected.

This new marriage of value creation and professional mission needs to be at the core of your growth strategies. And at least as important, it needs to be at the core of a plan to reverse the negative attrition trends reported by *IPA*. It's accounting's version of "cure the sick." And the sooner you make that public commitment to your employees and clients, the sooner you can begin to chip away at the human-capital drain that's sapping our talent pool and, as a result, our equity systems.

So our first commitment to practitioner-led value creation is needed to bind practitioners to one another in a properly motivated team, and our second commitment is to have all stakeholders lead the definition of quality in all our development initiatives. But our third—and perhaps most important—foundational commitment is what will direct your newly formed value-creation teams toward the mission of our profession.

And that target is big.

But We're Tired!

Leading accountants is not as easy today as it might have been a quarter century ago. The cynicism often bred among partners by repeated failed attempts to appeal to potential successors has left many of them jaded by the experience. They've grown suspicious and weary of the latest cheerleader's promise of a better and more meaningful future.

September's work-life balance initiative blends into the next busy season, which blends into the next summer's lightly attended business-development meetings, which blends into next September's cross-generational communication exercises, which blends into the approach of the next busy season.

Like the workings of a finely tuned Swiss watch, we slog from program to program every year, and without any greater definable accomplishment to show for our efforts than departmental revenue-growth bragging rights. That might be enough for departmental managers, but it's wholly inadequate for the troops they lead.

So without proper leadership and a solid cultural foundation in the first two commitments, your message of "we're going to build value-creation teams" conjures up agonizing images. When you say "value creation," your practitioners, partners, and nonpartners hear "more work." They've heard this before from every other flavor-of-the-month proposal about "voice of the customer," "customer-centric thinking," or the introduction of the mythological "CRM" creature.

Without establishing the appropriate cultural foundation, the choices of your practitioners look like this:

- Work more than their current 2,350 hours to make room for the dreaded extra work.
- Make room for the extra work, which they do not enjoy and aren't well suited for, by doing less specialist work, which they do enjoy and are well suited for.
- Nod politely in occasional leadership meetings about value creation, but abide by the daily leadership message of "bill your time."
- Leave public accounting.

None of these responses is an adequate foundation for the practitioner commitment that our Giants tell us is at the core of our succession crisis. "Work harder" is a fatally flawed leadership message in the absence of an important group goal. But where there *is* an important group goal, "work harder" is a natural, voluntary, and even unstoppable human response to the belief that your contribution is critical to achieving it. Just as Walmart needs "Save money. Live Better" to sustain a growing social contract between its workers and customers, so, too, do your CPAs and their clients need that missionary glue to sustain maximum commitment through good times and bad.

Where Do We Start?

So we're left wondering. The three foundational commitments make perfect sense. Let's bind our CPAs to one another in value-creation teams. Let's use a value-added standard to vet the building of our process systems. Then let's create a mission that marries value creation with the interests of all inside and outside stakeholders in business.

And what shall we do *after* lunch then, Paul?

Point taken. The potentially bottomless pit of expense we might see if we try to move too quickly from a hierarchical, specialist procedural-based profession to a collaborative, integrated outcome-based one is of grave concern to managing partners and boards of directors everywhere. The not-well-thought-out developmental efforts of the 1990s and 2000s are still hot-button issues for them. The notion of wandering off in the developmental woods without a solid implementation plan is a clear political nonstarter in board and management team meetings today.

I'm not going to lie to you and tell you it'll be easy. Nor will I tell you that it won't change the fundamentals of how you go about producing your products and services, because it will do so dramatically. But the happy news is that it won't cost you a dime more than you currently invest in development to make the transformation. You're already paying for it. So before we can start designing and building our new clinical practice systems, we need to reallocate costs to start getting them in line with economic trends.

You'll recall the discussion about how we've come to this crossroad that's already been experienced in many other professions, most demonstrably in medicine. As medicine did before us, we've come to the place where we can no longer simultaneously provide society with unlimited outcomes (or value) and also define quality on our own terms. We're simply too expensive now to have that luxury.

This is the same as saying we have enormous opportunity to reduce and eliminate non-value-added costs in our specialist production processes. Those processes not only don't provide value to our clients, but in many cases actually *cripple* our ability to produce the relevant information with an array of choices we'll need to create value with clients and serve stakeholder-accountability needs.

The only viable approach to firm development of this scale would have to include lean process engineering as a permanent guiding mechanism to ensure that unrecoverable production costs stop growing. The journey of moving away from indiscriminately building process systems that reflect our values as specialist accountants instead of those that reflect consumer needs will take choices.

So just as any great leader during difficult times, you'll need to characterize their sacrifices as being for the greater good of all. They cannot be viewed as a process of christening new political winners and losers in your firms. That's why you need a mission. We all need to be able to think of ourselves and our efforts as making an important contribution to a pressing joint professional goal of providing more relevance, transparency, and choices in the economy. And we all need to believe that the only way to accomplish this together is by providing more services to more people, more valuably, and at a declining cost.

The Simple Case

But before we head into a lean process discussion, I want to tell a story that illustrates the need for it. During the last few weeks of my practice days before I took a hiatus to write this book, one of my partner colleagues came to me to express her frustration with a particular process initiative. It seemed that our firm's leadership group that handled process development had made a decision to divert all of our client's general ledger data from all of its disparate sources into our internal processing environment's software.

Public accountants suffer a lot from dealing with their clients' proprietary software systems. It's much harder to uniformly produce our compiled, reviewed, and audited financial statement products if we allow all sorts of chaos to be going on at the end of earnings periods (i.e., months, quarters, years). This affects all sorts of efficiency requirements when taken from a departmental perspective.

So it makes some sense that redirecting all sources of client general ledger data into the one internal uniform solution at the firm would:

- Reduce our professional and administrative staff training burden
- Lead to a uniform and thus well-branded product offering
- Serve as a central storage area that would simplify future retrieval
- Reduce the amount of time required at year-end to redirect that information when we're very busy to get our tax returns and audits done

To accountants responsible for producing lots of a few particular products, the plan was unassailable. No one in their right mind would challenge such a thing, right? Well, my colleague *did,* based on one of her customer's needs, which was—you guessed it—transparency of relevant information with an array of choices the client needed to satisfy one of *his* organization's stakeholders.

My colleague's problem was that her client representative needed to be able to access his live data from our cloud-based general ledger solution at a time and way that was disrupted by the departmental plan to divert that information flow to our internal production systems. It turned out that he needed to prepare his departmental budget near the end of his fiscal year for submission to his board.

We'd quickly run smack into a predictable conflict between something our client valued and something we valued. It wasn't hard to predict who was going to win this battle. A lot of very hardworking accountants who operate under extraordinarily stressful conditions at certain times of the year are going to respond to every opportunity to streamline departmental production.

Cooperating Specialists

It's never easy for a partner to tell clients that they need to get in line occasionally for the wider good, but it does happen sometimes. The desire we all feel "to do things that just help the client," as our young CPA observed in Chapter 1, is compelling, but the story here seemed to be that the "good of the one" was trumped by the "good of the many." Politically, I sensed that this would be how it played out in any event.

But the example stuck with me as I contemplated my post-practice career of trying to help colleagues arrive at their preferred futures. Most of my career, I'd heard managers talk of how departmental "silos" were creating management problems. Specialization and the inevitable linear planning needed to support the production of large numbers of their procedures were clearly disruptive to our Giants' ability to create value as they had in the past.

The silos were also degrading our ability to provide the diversity of experience necessary to develop the firm's next generation of leadership. Their completely unrestrained response to specialization was no longer automatically producing managing partners with the breadth of experience necessary to address the more complex environments on the horizon.

We didn't like the bad parts of the silos, but we needed them—and they needed us. As long as billing rates could be adjusted upward as the cost of our labor rose, the numbers worked, and we could defer the value-creation challenges. Now, that challenge is no longer deferrable. And this moment has come at a time when funds available for investment in our firms' development are dwindling in the expense crunch undergone to keep partner incomes afloat.

My colleague's example would need to be looked at much more closely as I looked to make my case for lean process engineering in CPA firms. The challenge of providing more services, to more people, more valuably, and at a declining cost was no longer something I could dismiss as a disconnected series of departmental cost-management challenges. It was more complicated than that.

As our newly minted sales forces replaced our Finder Giants, and it became obvious that the activity of providing "more services to more people" was turning us into commodity-producing machines, I realized that the future foundation of our profession's profitability was contained elsewhere. It was the other half of Nick LaRusso's formula of managing the balance between "more valuably" and "declining cost" that contained the answer to our new business-leverage problem.

I needed to find a way to analyze my colleague's problem and present it to the rest of them in an accessible way, because it was a story being played out daily in accounting firms across the country. That analysis would take me not only to the immediate needs of our profession's near-term survival, but also to the gateway of our ultimate transformation into becoming the providers of the living, breathing, value-management infrastructure that the global business and investing community needs to make its best high-value, low-cost decisions.

Chapter 5

The Efficiency Equation

Having made the three commitments necessary to lay the foundation for solving the value-creation and commitment crises that the Giants told us about, we're now ready to start actually doing stuff to resolve them. It was important work getting here, though. We'll need those principles as a measuring stick for moving forward.

In times of unsettling change, people need principles to measure their progress rather than rules to follow. Rules are devised by a political process and, as such, are compromises. Principles, on the other hand, are not just guiding lights. They're immovable mountains that we cannot change. Together, these three commitments frame the ultimate picture of how our self-interest in a more rewarding professional life is unified with the moral imperative of doing the right thing for society.

As David Maister* observes in *Strategy and the Fat Smoker*,

> The necessary outcome of strategic planning is not analytical insight but resolve. If strategic rules are justified only in terms of outcomes ("exercise daily to look good"), (a) diet will always be seen as a punishment on the way to an uncertain and possibly unattainable reward. Accordingly, it will always be resented.

If we were only talking about our own work-life balance or the profitability of our firms, there wouldn't be the force of moral imperative needed to muster group resolve. Our three foundational commitments tell us that we need to

---

* Maister, David H. *Strategy and the Fat Smoker: Doing What's Obvious but Not Easy.* Boston: Spangle Press, 2008.

make a better life for ourselves *and* that it is the right thing to do for society. In short, if you haven't committed to these principles, you shouldn't bother with lean process engineering. Your CPAs will view you with suspicion and will resent your interference in their lives. And all you'll get along the way are more rules, regulations, and accommodations and a larger, more expensive, and less valuable way of practicing than you had when you started.

But even if you've made those commitments as a foundation for the idea of aspiring to provide more services to more people more valuably and at a declining cost, you won't have much political leeway. There will be serious leadership barriers to convincing practitioners that the way they instinctively provide services reduces value to their clients, makes their own lives miserable, and demotivates their successors.

Invariably, practitioners will view your process initiatives suspiciously. Either they'll see you as attacking their professional values by suggesting that their activities aren't valued by their clients, or they'll think you're attacking their chargeable time. That combination of feeling potentially devalued by an employer for lost chargeable time and a shrinking internal sense of self-worth could be fatal to even being able to discuss a lean environment. It'll look like a game of winners and losers to them, with them cast as the losers.

Save Money—Live Better

So we need a way to show our practitioners that the goal of lean engineering is not to devalue them and their efforts, but actually to help them feel more highly valued and secure in their customers' lives. In preaching value to my colleagues, I found that when I cast the argument from a CPA service provider's perspective, I got either blank stares or, if they were tracking with me, suspicious looks. But when I framed the value discussion from the perspective of being a *buyer* of professional services, they were able to divorce themselves from the provider role, and value creation made perfect sense.

For example, I'd tell the story of my shopping at Walmart for a pair of glasses. As I entered the store, the first thing I did was to glance at the frames on the wall. The technician was busy with another customer, so I busied myself browsing the frames. Of course, prices varied depending on style and material and whether they were full frames and such. If the process were truly one of simple consumption, I could have made my decision right then and there, with my wife deciding whether or not I'd made the correct fashion choice.

Of course, the process was a bit more complicated. While I knew that going in, I'm not an exceedingly patient sort, and sometimes the three-year-old boy in me comes out. That is, the thought of an eye exam didn't hold much allure after a long day at the office. Only later did it occur to me that I saw the eye doctor's services as almost an *impediment* to getting to my desired outcome, which was to see well and look good doing it. I'd have to sit still and answer questions, have little puffs of air blasted into my eyes, and read tiny letters. As an adult, I knew I couldn't avoid this part of the process. But that didn't make it any more attractive.

So—even though the process of the exam, writing of a prescription, visiting with the technician to choose frames and lenses, and then waiting for manufacture and fitting was inevitable—it struck me that the eye doctor's services were incidental to the overall value experience. In fact, for me, the highest value part of the visit was discussing my *array of available choices* with the technician.

As a tax professional, I thought of my services as central to the outcome of a resolved tax process. Yet my customers were probably thinking more like I was as a buyer of eyeglasses. To them, my tax preparation services were *incidental* to the outcome and not the other way around. That makes it easier to understand—and swallow, frankly—the notion of moving away from commodity procedure-based, specialty practice toward one of variably priced outcome-based practice. Looking at buying decisions through consumer eyes helps us see that we're not being attacked and that we're not alone as a profession in needing to deal with this. Most important, it tells us that the secret to increasing the fair-market value of what we do is not contained in our departmental processes. Rather, it's in the glue that binds all processes together into a human experience.

Being able to show case by case that we can develop plans to accomplish this together in value-creation teams will take daily, in-the-trenches management of practitioner concerns about the process. They'll wonder about the effect that lean process initiatives will have on how their firm values them and how they value themselves as professionals.

The increasingly politically decentralized nature of accounting firms (more voting partners) means that practitioner-led value creation can only take place voluntarily. You'll never be able to force it on them. So finding a way for them to see, feel, and touch it as they go is important to getting their voluntary—and eventually even enthusiastic—participation.

There's something of a dichotomy in knowing that the nature of accountants leads them to want to *quantify* things to assess them, but that the ultimate customer experience is one of subjective *quality* assessment. It was something of a challenge to come up with a process-evaluation metric system that contained both. But without a simultaneous process to account for both, our professional instincts would be to focus all of our energies on ways for our stakeholders to "Save Money" without ever really addressing how we could help them "Live Better."

The ultimate framework I arrived at occurred to me as I was mulling over the definition of the word *efficiency*. The dictionary defines *efficiency* as the ratio of the fair-market value of goods and services divided by the costs to produce that value. We can devise our process systems to influence the numerator or the denominator either positively or negatively. As accountants, of course, we typically gravitate to the denominator. It's much easier to identify and manipulate hard costs in the denominator than it is to measure fair-market value in the numerator, which is based in the much murkier "quality" concept.

So it's natural for us to focus on producing more of what we're already producing, but with equal or lower costs. And we assume this will lead to greater profitability, because our assumption is always that the numerator is a constant.

While we know this isn't true, as great convergent problem solvers, we also know it's much easier to make plans around a linear equation with only one variable than it is to have two or more variables. Despite the fact that our clients "don't value us the way that they used to" and "our services have become commodities," we haven't really tried to measure the numerator due to its subjectivity.

Not only do we gravitate to the denominator in the efficiency equation almost exclusively in our process efforts, we gravitate to our individual *processes' denominators* and completely disregard the *firm's aggregate numerator*. It is much easier for us to solve our linear production planning problems if we don't have to think too widely about the implications of our efforts outside our department. For the sake of simplicity and reducing the variables we have to deal with, we assume that our firm's aggregate numerator in the overall efficiency equation is simply an arithmetic sum of all our process numerators. And that assumption is dead wrong.

To test my new efficiency-measurement methodology, I returned to my colleague's Chapter 4 process problem. You'll recall that the firm's process initiative team members had determined that they would have far more efficient production of financial information if they diverted all general ledger information from all client sources into the firm's trial balance, financial statement production, and record storage solution.

As I understood it at the time, the group expected to achieve reductions in their processes' denominator, or labor costs, via the following:

- Reduced process variability
- Fewer software tools
- Less production process variance
- Uniform storage techniques
- Reduced output variability

It would be hard to argue with those goals taken in the context of my accounting colleagues' lives. I was a daily witness to how hard they work. And they're pressed to do ever more work during a smaller and smaller time window during each new busy season.

But my colleague's pain in not being able to serve her customer in the way her customer wanted to be served kept coming back to me. Was this really just a case of one outlying renegade that needed to get in line for the sake of the team? Or did this indicate a systemic value-creation problem to be addressed through process development?

I decided to put my money where my mouth was and test it against the new tools of the mission. How did my colleague's client's expressed needs stack up against them?

- Engagement
- Transparency
- Relevant information
- An array of available choices

Pretty well, it looked like. Client *engagement* was pretty evident in the fact that my colleague had been discussing the client's budgeting process, which was obviously important to him at the time. The client was concerned that he'd lose access to his general ledger data in the process adaptation, so *transparency* was important to him. Clearly, the information in question was *relevant,* because it was current and he needed to be able to update and present it to his *stakeholders* (his board) so that they could assess the *array of choices* he'd give to them in the budgeting process.

I'd tested the client's wishes and found them to fit the value-creation definition very neatly. It was far from being a request for exotic information within an unrealistic time frame. The client seemed more concerned that we not interfere with his own self-service efforts than he was about our processes. So it really didn't seem unreasonable to me. But a more telling picture was painted as I tested the firm's efficiency initiative against those same value-creation criteria.

The standard of accountant *engagement* seems to be pretty negatively affected by our process decision. The purpose of diverting the client information was actually to separate ourselves from our clients' live data. Clients live in far too messy a world for us, and public accountants' lives are improved dramatically when they can isolate themselves with a stable, unchanging set of data that they can manipulate to perfection. Unfortunately in the process, accountants lose their motivation to engage their customers in much more than inquiring about old data sets they're working on.

Transparency seems to be the most negatively affected. This one simple process move has created a uniform storage system for us, but it's also turned the information into accounting-firm property. And we know that, as such, we can't release that information without an act of the US Congress or, at a minimum, an engagement letter prohibiting clients from using it for anything without a letter of release from us. And it was originally the client's own property!

Relevance is, of course, in the eyes of the beholder, and it's a tricky standard. Relevance is very subjective and time sensitive, so we shouldn't presume to tell our clients what is or isn't relevant to their decision making. That's up to them. Our job should be to quickly and reliably retrieve or "make transparent" what our clients and third-party stakeholders believe to be relevant.

Our ultimate goal is to provide an *array of available choices* to our clients in an environment of engagement, transparency, and relevance. It's the place we want to live 365 days a year if we're on our value-creation toes. Nowhere in the initiative did I hear mention of a client choice, much less an array of them to choose from.

Having measured our clients' needs and the firm's process-development effort in the light of my newly combined value-creation and professional-mission scorecard, I was left with the clear belief that the firm's process initiatives needed better tools to help it discharge its duties to the firm and its clients.

With my balanced scorecard approach to process development, I'd found a way to continue to monitor hard process costs of each linear production line *and* weigh them along with the numerator in our firm's efficiency equation. I'd constructed a true efficiency analysis that could be used to quantify hard costs and assess quality as defined by our customers simultaneously.

Table 5.1   Linear Production Cost Analysis

Value	Costs
Increases:	Decreases:
	Linear training burden
Decreases:	Increases:

And because value-creation potential (founded in engagement, transparency, relevance, and an array of available choices) is also the foundation of our professional mission, our process initiatives can now employ the force of moral principle to muster practitioner resolve to act. The *Inside Public Accounting* observation about "giving your employees something greater to believe in"* inside your firms will be well served through lean process engineering if it's taken on for the right professional reasons.

But before we part company with our process initiative example, let's take a more quantitative look at our ratio of fair-market value divided by production costs. Before our lean analysis and our assessment of the effect on our firm's numerator, the ratio looks something like what is shown in Table 5.1.

In fairness, we should note that the intended linear production cost savings were handsomely achieved. We streamlined the training processes for record storage and retrieval, word-processing methods, analytical and presentation techniques, and managing quality control standards.

Unfortunately, one glaring result of the initiative was that trial balance work that had previously been considered to be bookkeeping was now considered to be compilation services. Information that previously belonged to the client had suddenly become the property of the firm, and, as such, was subject to federal privacy requirements and peer-review standards. So what was intended to be an overall benefit to the firm now looked like the scenario in Table 5.2 from a cost-management perspective.

What initially had looked like a professional and profitability win was starting to look like it might have been a loss. The true goal of "lean" is for everyone to win. Save Money. Live Better. No one noticed the firm-wide cost increases during the project's vetting phase. But it's understandable that folks working very hard in a highly focused manner will only see their department's needs. It's their job. It's their very important contribution to the firm's success.

---

* Platt Group. "National Benchmarking Report." *Inside Public Accounting*, 2011.

Table 5.2   Firm-Wide Cost Analysis

Value	Costs
Increases:	Decreases:
	Linear training burden
Decreases:	Increases:
	Peer review costs
	Work paper and financial reporting standards
	Insurance exposure

But if we're to accept the reality that the future of our profession is to become providers of business process infrastructure, we can no longer treat each of our linear production systems separately. In so doing, we wouldn't be able to build integrated business systems. We would only be able to produce commodities.

The lean process imperative tells us that the path toward providing "more services" to "more people" *must* start with providing our existing services "more valuably" and at a "declining cost" to integrate them successfully with everything else around them. When we move beyond the hard-cost analysis of our process initiative into the realm of value, as defined by our new tools of the mission, the picture is even bleaker (see Table 5.3).

One can, and should, argue that consistently prepared and compiled financial statements have value. But the real question is how we might provide that service in a way that maximizes value as perceived by all stakeholders. And it's guaranteed that we need practitioners who are actively engaged with customers in providing transparency of all relevant

Table 5.3   Firm-Wide Efficiency Analysis

Value	Costs
Increases:	Decreases:
	Linear training burden
Decreases:	Increases:
Disengagement	Peer review costs
Lack of transparency	Work paper and financial reporting standards
Irrelevance	Insurance exposure

information so that they can make their best decisions. Absent that engagement, we won't be able to rise above being seen by our clients as commodity service providers.

Now that we have a more complete definition of efficiency, we'll have a much more complete and useful way to approach process development. After all, we've committed to practitioner-led value creation. That job now belongs to us, and we can't delegate it to a sales force, administrative staff, or junior practitioners. And we've agreed that in pursuit of fulfilling that duty, we will have client perception of value guide our development activities. Having accomplished these things, we have done nothing less than aligned the goals of our clients, their stakeholders, and ourselves. No small accomplishment.

Let's measure ourselves right now against the yardstick of Nick LaRusso's idealized professional mission. Just like medicine, we, too, have now decided to become infrastructure providers responsible for integrated preventive health care and, most important, an increasingly valuable customer experience using the fewest possible resources. The only real difference is that we're going to treat business health rather than personal health. When we line up our criteria to measure our progress so far as firms, the situation looks something like what is depicted in Table 5.4.

The first column represents today's average accounting firm. The business-development gap left behind by the extinction of our Finder Giants has been largely defined as the ability to sell more stuff. It wasn't a conclusion without foundation, because historically, when accountants were cheap, large labor pyramids served to take care of business leverage for us no matter how inefficiently we used them.

The second column reflects the idealized professional mission of providing more services, to more people, more valuably, and at a declining cost. It's the path to becoming successful infrastructure providers. With our new

Table 5.4 Provider Market Position

Criteria	Provider			
	Commodity	Infrastructure	Minder-Giant	Niche
Provide more services	Y	Y	Y	N/A
To more people	Y	Y	Y	Y
More valuably	N	Y	Y	Y
At a declining cost	N	Y	N	Y

way to measure value and costs at the same time, we can now aspire to it, engineer for it, and lead our practitioners to it enthusiastically and happily.

The third column makes the point that we can't escape the value-creation and commitment challenge by returning to the Days of the Giants. Simply having the departing Giants turn the car keys over to willing and capable successor Giants won't get us to the promised land. The Giants could deliver value all right, but they couldn't do it today at a cost clients are willing to pay.

The last column illustrates a potential choice your firm can make, to be a niche provider of specialty services, say, tax preparation. It's a legitimate choice, and you can avoid a lot of headaches by choosing it. Providing "more services" to "more people" is a serious value-creation challenge that we shouldn't aspire to lightly. Now that we've looked at it critically, we know that value creation is more than a marketing statement to the effect that Using Our Expert Services = Your Company Happier.

The one constant that I found in talking with firms was that all of them are making strategic plans to grow. That was the one consistency in all firm models, regardless of size. Your permanent lean assessment teams, which are led by practitioners using the efficiency metrics in the previous example, will keep your firm in tune with where value is migrating and, as such, where growth is possible.

Growth, Stagnation, or Contraction?

I was chatting with a colleague one day about growth, and I observed that it was not untypical in my practice life to have what appeared to be a $25,000 tax return engagement be, in reality, a $5,000 tax return engagement with $20,000 worth of general-ledger-patching services. He agreed this was a fairly common scenario.

Many services we used to rely on for revenue had to do with providing after-the-fact services to a disjointed transactional world made worse by proprietary technology and specializing labor. That work is disappearing now, appropriately, and the void is being filled by integrated services that require little or no period-end correction.

And the labor that supported the after-the-fact work is disappearing at the same rate. US Bureau of Labor Statistics data tell us that the population of general-ledger bookkeepers has declined by 25 percent since 1985. The flattening of the technology curve means that this work will disappear at an even faster rate very soon.

So our biggest competitive threat is not presented to us by our colleagues next door and their expert tax preparation services. It's from transactional services that are merging vertically and migrating horizontally toward taking not your $5,000 tax return, but your $20,000 of after-the-fact infrastructure services.

It's pretty clear that lean engineering of our vertical, specialty-procedure production systems is only one step in our journey to the new business leverage that will support equity succession in the future. It's really only addressing how we process our $5,000 tax return. There's a whole lot more that needs to be done to protect or expand that other $20,000 in revenue.

But again, just as making our three foundational commitments were unavoidable steps to being able to conduct vertical lean engineering in our production systems, so, too, is that vertical production-engineering step necessary to lay the foundation for our next important step: to make a horizontal integration plan for each of our clients.

We can either embrace that hunt or withdraw from it into being specialty service providers with a much smaller piece of the pie than we had in the Days of the Giants. But if we choose to soldier ahead into the Days of the New Giants, we now must prepare for the horizontal integration of everything we do. It's not as hard as you might think, and the results can be quite pleasant and rewarding.

Chapter 6

Building Your Efficiency Numerator

I wish I had more original and less two-dimensional ways of referring to how my beloved profession's workplace activities interact to create and destroy value. If you successfully digested the Chapter 5 discussion about vertical lean process engineering, you deserve better treatment than to have me throw more MBA-speak at you. So, I promise to spend most of this chapter illustrating a true-to-life, live practice example of successful *horizontal lean integration* from my own days as a tax partner in a CPA firm.

The phrase "horizontal integration" never got much more response from me than wincing regret that I hadn't paid closer attention to the instructor that day in my business management class in college. It meant nothing to me until I eventually sought it out while I was trying to solve a set of tangible, real-life practice problems.

Before having such terms, I'd only been able to fumble with my intuitive beliefs about how our products worked (or didn't work) together very valuably. Since intuition is internal and can't be easily conferred on others, I needed terms, examples, and a prescription to follow to try to help my colleagues significantly improve their professional lives.

Up until now, we've been laying the foundation both politically and culturally in our firms to return to the value-creation practice we'll need to create the Days of the New Giants. The three market commitments made it possible for us to start conducting lean engineering in our vertical production systems (e.g., tax returns and audits) to free up resources to take the next step in our journey to solving the succession crisis in public accounting.

And that next important step, which all of this preparation has made you ready for, is to make a horizontal integration plan for each and every client served by your firm. The happy news is that there are lots of ways to do this, and your integration plan doesn't need to look like anyone else's. The important thing is that, at the end of the day, you can measure your client-service approach by the two important yardsticks we established in the commitment process.

Nick LaRusso taught us that any profession's overarching *goal* needs to be to provide more services, to more people, more valuably, and at a declining cost. The *means* test, which is unique to our profession, measures if we've accomplished this by *engaging our client* to try to *make all relevant information transparent,* so that stakeholders can make their best risk-based *choices.* Now let's take a look at one small example of what that horizontal integration plan might look like in the real world.

The Dreaded Fee Discussion

A couple of years ago, one of those dreaded communications arrived in my e-mail inbox. A very likable client of our firm was letting me know in his own indirect way that our accounting fees were getting past his comfort level, particularly in view of the Great Recession and its effects on his charitable organizations. His was a messy little accounting project that involved two small legal entities: a public charity and a private foundation. The public charity had gross receipts of around $1 million, and the private foundation's invested assets were around $6 million.

The public charity had an audit requirement because its revenues were in excess of $500,000. But it was not an overly complex accounting engagement, other than some fairly complicated tax return preparation requirements for private foundations. The fees we were charging the client are shown in Table 6.1.

Table 6.1 Accounting Firm Annual Fees

Service	Fees ($)
Public charity audit and tax return	14,385
Private foundation tax return	7,590
Total	*21,975*

Armed with this information, and a general sense of how the workflow was conducted in my firm and inside his own office, I called my good client to talk with him and his son about our year-end accounting fees. Our conversation went something like this:

Bill: Paul, I'm having a hard time understanding how the fees for the foundation could be $7,500. We only write a couple of checks per month. Your folks could personally record 100 percent of them with very little effort.

While I knew the source of inefficiency had nothing to do with check writing or recording, rather than saying so outright, I started the following line of inquiry:

Me: Bill, how many money managers do you have?

Bill: Three.

Me: Okay, imagine a world where we receive thirty-six month-end brokerage statements issued by those three investment houses in February. Your bookkeeper is very thorough and wouldn't want to burden us with an incomplete set of information during the year. So he holds onto all of the documents until the set is complete after year-end so that he can send them all at once. Then, right during our busiest production time of the year, a supervisor assigns a junior accountant to summarize that information by separate spreadsheet analysis. We have to do that to put all of that previous year's activity and those ending balances into debit- and credit-ready form. I knew a while ago that this wasn't a very efficient arrangement, so a few years back I asked your bookkeeper to summarize that information during the year before sending it to us. He made it clear to us that he wasn't comfortable doing that, because he hadn't been trained in certain techniques involving the stock trades and unrealized gains and losses. He was really only comfortable reconciling cash activity.

There were murmurs of recognition as I painted that all-too-familiar picture of accounting firm production even after the advent of the Great Recession. Bill knew instinctively that his costs were entirely controllable if he was willing to address the barriers to efficiency inside his own office. So I summarized the primary cost-effectiveness issues in his particular Everything-Else Department, that process infrastructure whose job it is to support fundraising and grant making:

- Work was being deferred until after year-end due to internal capability limitations.
- Money management services were overpriced due to decentralization.
- Transactional work was being performed multiple times.
- Fragmented service providers allowed no bundled pricing.
- There was excessive labor-mediated data movement.

And I ended our phone call as follows:

Me: Bill, we both have labor working in your organization. The reality is that we need to manage an infrastructure jointly across the borders of our organizations. Accounting has been inexpensive enough historically that we didn't need to worry about putting much effort into that. But now that technology and specialization have made accountants so expensive, it needs to be more formally addressed.

With your permission, I'd like to take a look at the overall cost of your accounting and administrative function and illustrate where some of the value-creation opportunities might be.

Painting the Picture

Bill and his son certainly had nothing to lose by listening, so they sent me on my fact-finding and analytical mission. And here is what I found (see Table 6.2). The $88,875 represents the grand total of wages and fees paid to my accounting firm, our client's bookkeeper, an external payroll provider, and three investment managers. Our accounting firm had about 25 percent of that total, of which nearly 100 percent was conducted between January 1 and May 31 of the calendar year, our busy season.

It was clear that there were pretty serious inefficiencies that arose from my firm's accountants needing to perform basic work after year-end that could have been easily performed during the year. We weren't going to be able to charge premium emergency room prices after year-end for what should have been inexpensive clinical work during the year. But that wasn't the whole problem.

There were even more serious efficiency issues related to complex audit and tax regulations. Our nonprofit-specialist audit partner performing the year-end services had noted several pretty serious compliance issues. The client's employee in charge of investments had made some decisions that fell

Table 6.2   Current Infrastructure Costs of Administrative and Account Functions for a Public Charity and a Private Foundation

	Public Charity ($)	Private Foundation ($)	Total ($)
Bookkeeping services—internal	8,640	1,800	10,440
Payroll services—external	960	–	960
Investment management services	–	55,500	55,500
Financial statement analysis, closing, and document production	5,385	3,590	8,975
Audit services	5,000	–	5,000
Tax preparation services	4,000	4,000	8,000
Total costs ($)	**23,985**	**64,890**	**88,875**

outside the rules for what was permitted. He didn't do so intentionally; he just didn't know what the rules were during the course of the year.

Those compliance problems were a serious irritation to my nonprofit-specialist partner, and justifiably so. It's very frustrating to try to push mass quantities of work through a shrinking pipeline and have compliance problems arise that could have been easily avoided with only minimal attention during the course of the year. It's easy to see at compensation time that he would feel he should be paid *extra* for having to suffer such irritation, not *less* like the client was thinking.

A Serious Value-Creation Problem

No one was happy with me. The client felt overcharged. Our nonprofit specialist felt unnecessarily alarmed, pressured, and unappreciated. The internal bookkeeper felt threatened. It was right then that I began to consider the potential benefits of an occupation in business book authorship rather than relationship partner in an accounting firm.

At first it seemed like a daunting task. How the hell was I going to provide more services to a client who felt overcharged to begin with? On top of that, it was hard to imagine having a successful conversation with my audit partner colleague about reducing costs while he was already feeling undervalued and frustrated with compliance issues he felt were entirely avoidable.

Unhappily, I didn't have my "means test" prescription available to me at the time and was operating solely on instinct. In retrospect, though, I could have simply hauled out my chart for guidance. Were we engaged sufficiently? No. Was there transparency of all relevant information? Not really. We were backpedaling most of the time. Did we put our client and its stakeholders in a position to make their risk-based decisions? No. We weren't even close. And we were making ourselves miserable in the process.

I'd failed everyone involved and failed my professional mission, and it was time to do something about it. Instead of wringing my hands, I set to thinking about each element of our client's Everything-Else Department and what I might be able to do to reduce costs and increase value in it.

I'd need to take a whole new look at the structure of the client's and our own internal technology capabilities. Having two different entities build their own technology systems without consulting one another, and at the same time, tacitly agreeing to jointly provide a business process infrastructure, wasn't going to pass muster any longer. We'd have to cooperate in some way to get to the goal.

We'd need to think about shrinking the number of service providers to streamline labor-mediated data movement. Due to specialization and unit-of-output productivity, gone were the days of accounting firm personnel being inexpensive carrier pigeons in and among a disjointed set of service providers. We were just too expensive for that now, and I needed a plan that took that reality into account.

I knew I'd need a new standard of client care that started with engagement, transparency, relevance, and providing choices to clients and society, rather than independence as the foundation for considering my firm's value-creation potential. And if that standard of client care interfered with my firm's ability to audit clients because I'd violated independence rules, I'd need to make my choices in full knowledge of all the possibilities instead of "editing myself" in advance of arranging services.

I decided to look at technology first. The client's internal accountant used a general ledger software that had two problems with it:

■ The software package had little market penetration. Almost no one used that software any more, so it was a barrier to our being able to help during the year.
■ The software was not a cloud-supported product, which simply compounded the first problem. We needed a cloud-computing solution so that our accountants could provide contemporaneous assistance.

As it was, no one could help the poor fellow get his work done correctly the first time, and—even if we knew how to operate his proprietary software system—someone would have to drive downtown to help.

So whatever software solution we recommended, it would need great market penetration, be very easy to use, and have a cloud-based interface, or some combination of those attributes. All of these things together would make it possible to find and use labor from anywhere in the world. Whatever the ultimate labor solution, it was clear that leaving an untrained, unsupervised employee working for a year inside a proprietary technology infrastructure that was insulated from the outside world wasn't going to be a part of a value-oriented solution.

For the illustration, I assumed that our firm would perform the transactional services previously handled by the part-time bookkeeper. One of my main assumptions was that work during the year had to be done in a way that minimized, or eliminated, year-end adjustment. I could only reliably commit to that if I could control those inputs during the year.

But as I looked at the numerator, or fair-market value of our work, I spotted what would get us to the real prize of reducing costs and not just *maintaining*, but *increasing* the value of our services. In this new arrangement where we controlled the inputs, my hardworking, talented audit partner should be able to review accounting and financial information on a timely basis and make recommendations that could avoid the audit findings in the first place.

When I looked at the time taken for research, internal consultation (i.e., appropriately upbraiding the relationship partner), and agonizing over the compliance issues addressed in the audit, it was easy to see that we could reduce those costs to a small fraction of what they were in our current arrangement.

But as I noted earlier, the compliance problem wasn't the checks written on the general cash account. Evidence of the nonpermissible investments was contained in the brokerage statements furnished by the three investment houses. Financial services were my next horizontal integration opportunity.

A quick look at the fees paid for financial services fees showed that our client was being charged around 1 percent of asset values for money-management services in the private foundation. This would have been reasonable fair-market value if you took $6 million and split it among the three providers.

But, like in any industry, volume purchasing has its benefits. Percentages charged as a money-management fee are reduced as an asset base under management gets larger. Whereas a $1-million portfolio might go for 1 percent of assets, a $6-million portfolio might only be charged 0.65 percent. Our client was significantly overpaying for money-management services by splitting the work among three service providers.

It was right then that I recalled a discussion I'd had with Bill about financial services several years before. As a good tax partner in the firm, I'd wanted to let our client know that we also provided financial services and see if I could get a shot at the work. At the time, my motivation was strictly self-interest; that is, I had no other reason to ask for that business other than to get more of it for my firm. I even arranged for Bill to meet with our providers of those services and followed up later with a call.

So I asked Bill if he'd consider giving us the financial services work. His tepid response was that he'd be willing to give us "some" of that work. Because he'd emphasized the word "some," I politely declined. It didn't really sound like we could add value or like it was anything he felt he needed. He was simply responding to me as was his nature, wanting to be a nice guy who was good to his friends. But it seemed to me like chopping the foundation's financial services into even littler bits wasn't in its best interests, although I couldn't really verbalize why at the time.

But now we were looking at lean horizontal integration of financial services into an overall value-creation assessment of our client's Everything-Else Department. We could add serious value and reduce serious hard costs while serving our professional mission better. It was the win-win-win situation I knew existed and that we now needed to unearth, since the Great Recession had begun demanding more value at a lower cost.

Armed with this mission, I went to our financial services department and asked about our technology capabilities. Would we be able to provide the investment management services and also have the accounting debits and credits produced contemporaneously? Could that information then be sent directly to our cloud-based general ledger software so that everyone had access to it during the year? I was assured that this would be doable, and we assessed the cost of those services internally.

I suddenly realized that, unlike the last time we talked about financial services, this time my motivation wasn't to get more business for my firm but, rather, to better serve our client's needs. This "Whose best interests are being served?" question will be a critical one—and one you'll need to manage if you want to motivate your New Giants to provide more services to more people.

Without the mission, most of your practitioners will view their role in the call to provide more services to more people as one of carnival barker. With the new mission in place and leading the way, practitioners will view your leadership appeal as a call to exalted professionalism. They'll be cast in the natural and desirable roles of problem solvers rather than shills for your firm's ancillary services.

At this point in analyzing our client's Everything-Else Department, I'd addressed bookkeeping, payroll services, and financial services. I'd consulted with my colleagues on prices for those services and then reallocated costs to illustrate the separation of tax return services from audit services from everything else.

The main pricing benefits had come from (1) bundling of services, (2) addressing transactional services to make them high quality and contemporaneously performed, and (3) including my specialist audit partner's services for periodically reviewing investment and other compliance issues during the year. In doing so, my plan was to eliminate the expensive, frustrating audit work that produced negative findings that no one wanted in the year-end report.

As a result of all of this good and necessary work, it was obvious that we wouldn't be doing the audit work under this arrangement. After-the-fact auditing rules appropriately prohibit parties-in-interest who might be the subject of audit findings from performing the work that would produce those findings. That's the common-sense conflict-of-interest foundation of our profession's independence rules. So that work would have to be outsourced to another firm specializing in nonprofit auditing. The final analysis looked something like what is shown in Table 6.3.

In our projection, overall costs of our client's Everything-Else Department had been reduced by over 22 percent. Also, despite the fact that a small audit would be lost to a competitor, our firm was positioned for a 200 percent increase in revenues. The client and our firm's specialist colleagues, with a little prodding from me, had come up with a service proposal that provided our services far *more valuably* and at a substantially *declining cost*. As we discussed in Chapter 5 on vertical lean processes, this is a very necessary first step to being able to provide *more services* to *more people* and complete the goal portion of Nick LaRusso's good advice to us.

Table 6.3 Proposed Infrastructure Costs of Administrative and Account Functions for a Public Charity and a Private Foundation

	Public Charity ($)	Private Foundation ($)	Total ($)
Bookkeeping services—internal	–	–	–
Bookkeeping services—external	8,640	1,800	10,440
Payroll services—external	790	790	1,580
Investment management services	–	39,800	39,800
Financial statement analysis, closing, and document production	3,230	1,000	4,230
Audit services	5,000	–	5,000
Tax preparation services	4,000	4,000	8,000
Total costs ($)	**21,660**	**47,390**	**69,050**

But Did We Win the War?

So everyone should be happy now. Our client's costs are reduced. Our audit partner is off the hook for emergency-room compliance diagnostics at the busiest time of the year. All of our transactional service providers are working efficiently and happily. We've met the final test, and we're done now, right?

Not quite. The fact that costs are low and value is high makes for a compelling story. But the Walmart example has taught us that it isn't just about the money. It's about pursuing a higher purpose that contributes to a wider societal good. So lastly, we need to compare our new proposed service arrangement with the new means to meet our professional mission.

If the new arrangement fits those criteria, then we know our proposed new business contract has been properly expressed as a socioeconomic necessity. We know now that traction between our firms and our clients needs to be about more than them consuming as many of our offerings as they possibly can. We need to have our economic transactions elevated to the status of social imperative—certainly at least as much as Walmart does.

When we first looked at the criteria of engagement, transparency, relevance, and choices in our service pattern, I was failing miserably. I needed to fix that. I was keenly aware that my job was not just to figure out a way to illustrate that "the client is always right," as I'd done in my days as one of the soon-to-be-extinct Minder Giants, but I needed to solve the equation on behalf of my colleagues as well.

For starters, the *engagement* of our CPA practitioners and support personnel in the new arrangement was pretty impressive. CPA busy-season workload had been reduced by 45 percent, despite tripling our annual revenue. We couldn't have accomplished that with personnel performing most of their services after year-end. Nor could we have done so without addressing the need for horizontal connection between those services during the year in our own firm's offices. Perhaps the most important engagement improvement, frankly, had to do with practitioner connectedness to one another, as opposed to client engagement.

Transparency was a clear winner because our client's financial information would now be continuously available to our client personnel, our specialist CPAs, and any third-party stakeholder our client chose (or was required) to share information with. Our new work arrangement had moved substantial resources away from periodic after-the-fact correction to real-time services.

One major property influencing *relevance* is, of course, time. We know that regardless of content, information's relevance to today's decision making declines as time passes. And we know that the informational half-life of relevance is shrinking rapidly today because of globalization. So whatever our clients and stakeholders tell us is relevant will only be so for smaller and smaller periods of time as globalization continues to make our world smaller.

In that future world, anything less than truly real-time availability of relevant metrics will not provide any value at all. Our proposed arrangement with the client, while only dealing with relevant financial statement reporting right now, puts us in a position to begin looking for those relevant metrics as our clients and their stakeholders decide what they are and tell us that they want them.

At a minimum, our client's *array of available choices* has been expanded considerably. Armed with new information about investment choices, the client minimizes or eliminates the risk of making choices not in compliance with laws and regulations. That was the firm's biggest cost driver and its biggest value impairment, so solving that one was very important. And as more and more relevant business metrics are uncovered, our practitioners will now be deployed in a real-time environment that far better positions them to help with expanding those value-generating choices.

I'd now satisfied myself that our analysis served the *goal* of our profession as well as used the new *means* of serving that mission. We'd constructed a scenario that provided more services to more people, more valuably, and at a declining cost. And we'd done so by structuring our technology and activity infrastructure to be engaged enough to provide transparency of relevant information so that our client could make its best risk-based choices.

Oh, and by the Way

I saved one part of the analysis for last and for a really big reason. It can't have escaped any reader's notice that our practitioners in this future world will have a far better life. Our new arrangement reduces CPA busy-season workload by 45 percent. It also elevates the role of our nonprofit specialist to one of value-added advisor, helping with the important decisions of today instead of the role of killjoy-snitch during the audit process.

I saved that observation to reiterate a very important point about the motivational linkages that must be in place before asking accountants to move together in a new and uncertain direction. We make an enormous, and fatal, mistake when we tell our practitioners that the primary purpose of our strategic initiatives is to help them achieve a better work–life balance. There's nothing more damaging to a leader's credibility than to lie to practitioners about this, although not for the reasons you might think.

David Maister's observation about "the diet" in *Strategy and the Fat Smoker* is the real reason.* When we tell our CPAs that they should sell more services so they don't have to prepare as many tax returns and audits, we're falling into a serious motivational trap that Maister warns us about: justifying strategy only in terms of outcomes. "Sell more other services to our clients so you won't have to prepare so many tax returns" is Maister's "punishment on the way to an uncertain and possibly unattainable reward." In effect, we'd be telling practitioners that if they swallow this dreadful medicine of shilling products, then maybe they won't have to work so hard in their own specialties. And they will resent it—a lot.

If the urgent need for us to provide more services to more people, more valuably, and at a declining cost is expressed as necessary to fulfill an important societal mission, we're much more likely to be successful in

---

* Maister, David H. *Strategy and the Fat Smoker: Doing What's Obvious but Not Easy.* Boston: Spangle Press, 2008.

gaining traction with our specialist practitioners. The urgency to engage society in this way has the full weight of a moral imperative. Enhancing transparency, relevance, and choices by engaging better with their clients is the *right thing to do*. The positive work–life-balance outcome is frankly only a natural by-product of striving to accomplish the mission. People actually want to work harder, but generally only for the right reasons.

So armed with my analysis, I trotted off to make a presentation of the proposal to Bill and his son. They listened politely and nodded at the appropriate times throughout the discussion. They very quickly assimilated the information and agreed that there was a compelling argument for adapting to an outsource model as the foundation for managing the Everything-Else Department for all of the good reasons I laid out. So naturally they accepted the proposal and agreed to the restructuring, right?

Unfortunately, not right then. Making that move would have involved terminating relationships with service providers (the part-time bookkeeper and Bill's friends in the financial services industry), with whom he had relationships spanning decades. The loyalties he felt for these people were simply too strong to overcome with an efficiency argument. And I admire his loyalty.

But the effort undergone to analyze their business process infrastructure was productive for several reasons. First, Bill and his son could now take responsibility for their accounting firm fees, because they'd declined a much better deal. In the end, having a quieter client would have made my life easier, but the cost would have been to have a client silently feeling overcharged and specialist colleagues quietly feeling overworked and underappreciated. This would not be a good succession environment for our New Giants.

The cost reallocation from procedural specialty services to horizontal integration services happened in our example just the way it needs to happen in your offices if you're to have a realistic hope of laying the growth foundation you need. Those two permanent mechanisms built into your daily processes will now put you in a position to motivate your New Giants to remain onboard along with expanding client relationships.

You're Not Alone

It's not only a very real practical outcome of the marriage of value and professional mission; it's also the connection between the succession crisis looming in our profession and the one happening in our clients' offices. Similar to the vice president of internal audit I spoke of earlier, here was another instance in which the available resources of an accounting firm matched up well with a client's need to manage single-point-of-failure risk and process scalability that would provide for succession in his own Everything-Else Department.

Were they really one and the same? Was there a natural extension from the mechanics of transactional services and their informational output into building a sustainable, non-labor-dependent, value-creation process for our customers? If we could solve our own value-creation crisis, might we actually be laying the foundation for becoming a part of the succession solution for business?

I decided it was worth a look in any event. So I started interviewing customers of my accounting firm whom I'd previously served in the role of "relationship manager"—that murky function sometimes referred to as Minder, or Customer Relationship Manager (CRM), or person-who-doesn't-actually-do-anything. Or my own personal favorite, Professional Eater.

What I learned was that our succession problems weren't all that unique. The whole world, it seemed, was populated with nearly departing Giants who were waiting for the New Giants to take the keys to the value-creation car and drive it along the same old roads.

And the sound of crickets chirping in their offices was deafening.

Chapter 7

Succession Is Everyone's Crisis

The job of relationship manager in an accounting firm is a strange one indeed. Until recently, it was still reasonably efficient to conduct all sorts of services after year-end in far-less-than-valuable ways and then to employ someone to come in afterward and ask, "Did everything go okay?"

The notion that we should design the performance of our services to hit the biggest value target possible the first time was preposterous. It was cheap and easy to push lots of tax returns and audits through our busy seasons and then have political partners massage the value equation by engaging with a relatively unchanging body of deciders in summer and fall. A few lunches, theater outings, and schmoozy meetings later, and value had been maintained for yet another year.

We even shamed ourselves into thinking that concerning ourselves with value creation right in the middle of our service delivery of audits and tax returns might run afoul of our mission. Gosh, if we focused on value, we might not be independent! If we treated our clients as though they should feel good about our work, we wouldn't be objective!

Of course, this attitude mischaracterizes value creation in a very fundamental way. There is absolutely nothing inherently unethical about "engagement, transparency, relevance, and choices." They are actually highly ethical principles and goals. We only have a problem when "choices" morphs into "conspiracy to make illegal choices" or "engagement" grows into "conflict of interest."

The Minder's Lament

I remember a particular client's response when I told him I was going to take a break from active practice to write a book. He purchases a lot of services from our firm, and I assured him that he should expect to continue to receive high-quality services after I was gone. After all, I really didn't do anything on his account other than stop in occasionally after the dust settled to ask, "Did everything go okay?"

He seemed annoyed. He'd come to rely on our relationship to produce advice. "That's where the value is!" As much as I wanted to blush modestly, thank him for the compliment, and leave the meeting with that warm post-affirmation glow that only a true narcissist with a leaky self-worth bucket could properly appreciate, I was suddenly worried. Was that really it? Was I leaving behind nothing more than that?

I'd felt that fear before in observing the departure of Minder Giants, but it seemed different now. And it seemed different not because it was now my turn to leave, but because there weren't enough remaining new Minder Giants to go around. What used to be ten aspiring Minders competing to replace one retiree now looked like the exact opposite.

And what was even more frightening was the fact that there were similarly few, and rapidly aging, purchasers of service in our clients' offices to sustain another attempted repetition of next-generation Minder replacement. Those Giants in our clients' offices had fewer successors, too, due to specialization and productivity. And that combined effect of having a single-point-of-failure relationship risk on both sides of the transaction didn't seem to bode well for the continuation of client relationships or, at a minimum, the future of value pricing based on relationships.

The continuity of a lot of purchasing of professional services that was passed from Finder to Minder to Grinder in the Days of the Giants through long-standing political relationships seemed like it might soon come to a screeching halt. Neither side of the buying transaction had a labor pyramid to organically pass those relationship torches down to the next generation. So something other than the traditional labor-mediated, value-management handoff to another generation of Minder Giants would likely be needed for business continuity.

It was now painfully obvious that it was no longer about the Giants letting go of the value-creation car keys or the New Giants picking them up. Those fewer, more specialized New Giants would need a far more efficient vehicle than I'd driven to successfully create value *and* provide for succession of that capability over time on this kind of scale.

The Merger of Value and Succession

So while I'd been agonizing about where the new Minders were coming from, the creation of value and the maintenance of that capability over time, or its *succession,* had merged to become "value management." They were no longer two things, but one. Systematic value management had become my challenge and, most important, *it was our customers' big challenge too.*

One of our clients asked about the premise of my book one day at lunch. I began by explaining Dr. Ofri's description of older physicians' tales of woe about modern medical practitioners and how those stories correlated to ones I'd heard from my own colleagues. I wasn't more than a minute into the premise when he exclaimed, "That's *my* problem!"

He went on to give a litany of complaints about his employees' lack of entrepreneurialism, disinterest in working after business hours, ambivalence toward client social interaction, unwillingness to meet unique customer needs, and a generally dismissive attitude about all of the things Minder Giants do to patch the value wagon together on a daily basis.

He felt like he was the only Giant left in his business who understood what it took to run it. He knew the things his customers wanted, and he knew how to provide them using the resources on hand. And he was a good motivator of employees, so he didn't have too much trouble keeping them moving toward better customer service.

But his employees were more specialized now. He'd recognized the change that had taken place over the last quarter century. It was no longer, "If you've got the work, you can get the people." Now it had become, "If you've got the people, you can get the work." Those employees were all mission-critical in their own way and had become fundamentally "untouchable," much to the consternation of the head of operations of my friend's business.

The production people, the sales people, the technology people—all had an increasingly unique and hard-to-replace feature such that value creation had become my client's daily personal task. Unlike the dry-eyed accountability-focused operations manager in charge of driving the operational train, my client's function was more of marionette puppeteer, alternately cajoling, cheering, wining, dining, and threatening his way through his daily value-creation duties with the few remaining denizens of his value-creation universe. He was the only Minder Giant left, and there was no successor in sight.

Interestingly, though, the fact that there was no successor in sight wasn't of grave concern to him. In fact, he was having fun being the head Minder Giant, and I envied him just a little at that moment. It *was* fun to be the head Minder Giant, but, unlike my client, I had a broad and diverse share-holder population back at the firm that I was responsible to. I couldn't just sit there enjoying my inefficient role, occasionally stopping to lament that no one knew quite how to do it like I did back in the Days of the Giants.

Both my profession *and* my client's business had serious value-management problems. Both of our value-creation systems were far too inefficient to be portable to yet another generation of Minder Giants, even if those creatures still roamed the earth. And despite that reality, neither of us had even really begun to construct the new value-management systems we both needed to ensure continuity and growing shareholder value after our departures.

I had to admit that the fact that my client was experiencing the same problem as I was a bit of a relief. Misery loves company, and it would provide even more grist for our "Gee, things sure ain't the way they used to be" lunchtime visits. There's always that temptation to enjoy the guilty pleasure of crotchety-old-man-phoning-it-in-until-retirement syndrome.

Two Birds with One Stone

As I thought more about it, I came to think there might be a contribution that my profession could make to my client's value-management problem. And even more remarkably, I came to believe we could make that contribution *as a by-product of solving our own value-management problem.* The story of my Chapter 4 friend, the head of internal audit at a small publicly traded company, describes that opportunity very tidily.

In that example, contracting my friend's position to one of their accounting firms (only theoretically, of course, because my friend wants to keep his job, and I want to keep him as a friend) would be a huge plus in my profession's column. That accounting firm would get to use that position to create a collaborative, interdisciplinary team inside its own walls, which our New Giants tell us is good for practitioner commitment. We know now that those brave new accountants want to participate in the decision-support function at every opportunity.

My friend's company wins, too, because it no longer needs to manage the scalability of its internal audit function. It can let an outside accounting firm take care of that now instead of attempting to grow a department-of-one to a bustling growth-filled future. This leaves the company free to allocate more of its full-time labor to the business of creating value. After all, synthesis and integration of core competencies is the only *real* value-creation challenge, isn't it? And that's just not what accountants are all about, is it? As it turns out, maybe it should be.

My internal auditor friend later updated me on his story. I wanted to confirm something I thought I'd heard him say in a previous visit about his value-creation duties at his company. My friend patiently explained to me that his department had been charged with the goal of making recommendations that *added value* to his company's production processes. As an ex-tax partner, I don't want to pretend to have the expertise of an internal auditor, but I think it's safe to say that historically it was mostly about the design, implementation, and maintenance of systems intended to prevent waste, fraud, and abuse.

Another way of expressing it was that his department historically was concerned with waste and fraud in the *denominator* of his company's *cost* structure. Now, my friend was being asked if he could help enhance the *numerator* of his company's *value-creation performance*. This sounded a lot like the efficiency discussion we needed to have in our own value-creation efforts in the previous chapter.

As an example, he told me about his auditors' dissection of their shipping policies and practices. The company was having problems related to products that were arriving late to retail outlets. In addition, there was more container damage than was acceptable to the company's customers. One can imagine what sort of effect that might have on customer satisfaction as reflected in surveys or, more publicly, in online Internet reviews.

So he was asked if his auditors could look into it and see what could be done. Both issues—damaged containers and the lateness of the shipments—were concerned with managing the value perception of customers. Neither of them fell into the traditional waste, fraud, and abuse efforts of internal auditors, whose job was geared more toward avoiding hard-asset waste.

My friend did admit that, although his auditors succeeded in solving both value issues for his employer, he wasn't overly excited about engaging in the task at first. The expertise involved with logistics and package design was not something he'd been trained for. They were specialized functions. But because his was a relatively small publicly traded company, there really wasn't anyone else around to take the reins. So he agreed to give it his best shot.

The solution, which substantially reduced the company's two value problems, involved packaging the product in containers, packing the containers on the trucks, delivering them to retail outlets, and orienting the packages inside the truck. Small contributions of expertise from a broad range of fields were needed to synthesize a solution for what turned out to be a relatively straightforward problem.

This illustrates a typical problem that can go unnoticed in our age of high-productivity expectations and specialization demands. For example, there are very specialized people employed in this company whose job it is to engineer packaging. And there are people employed who oversee the logistics of product movement through the company and out to the consumer. Not only are they all experts in their fields, but the productivity demands of the Great Recession mean there are far fewer specialists now, and each one is doing far more work.

So, as highly motivated experts in their fields, they spend their days agonizing over every aspect of the "big things" associated with their specialized contributions to the company. The smaller things—if containers are damaged in shipment due to poor logistical controls, for example—are someone else's problem. They can't solve what they can't control.

The folks in logistics can tell you the same story. There are a million compelling reasons why the products simply must be delivered in the manner that they are. If only packaging would come up with a design that was more adaptive to real-world needs, the world would be a much better place. It's easy to see how, similar to our own value-management problems, business processes of all kinds suffer from a lack of integrative capacity.

When I inquired again about that story at a later visit, my friend remembered it. I'd now identified the potential of the story as an example in my post-practice work and wanted to confirm it with him. While he did confirm it, I sensed even more reticence on his part to embrace the whole notion of value management through the exercise of integration skills in his internal audit department.

It turned out that after that one successful foray into multidisciplinary collaboration, the company asked him for more value-management work. Many of those requests apparently got too far afield from his core competencies for him to be comfortable. He'd been trained, after all, as an internal auditor and was properly concerned that he or his junior charges had sufficient knowledge of underlying specialties to do a good job. So he began declining those opportunities out of concern for quality control.

Happy Retirement!

Consider now that future world where my friend is safely retired and his former employer is faced with a decision to replace him. The company now knows that what it wants from its internal audit function is evolving from a relatively static need for traditional services that protect the company's hard assets from theft and waste. That function is now moving to a model that increasingly asks for dynamic value-management services—or "decision support"—aimed at protecting physical capital *and* growing intellectual capital.

And the company has recognized the macroeconomic principle of allocative efficiency and its effects on that department that are drawing resources away from traditional accounting functions. The economy needs these resources to fund its new intellectual-capital maintenance capability provided by engagement, transparency, relevance, and choices. Traditional hard-asset protection is still a vital function, but it will have to meet its objectives with fewer resources.

So the company has a math problem. Will it be worth paying the overhead of an outsourced service provider to fill the position? Or will the company's needs be more cost-effectively served by hiring a full-time internal audit specialist? Of course we don't have enough specific information to answer that question from the comfort of our armchairs. But we do have enough trend information about the competing economic constraints to start to line up a decision-making process.

One or the Other?

Our illustrative company has traditionally had a department head and a few employees. In Chapter 4, we learned that those few direct reports were no longer permanent occupants of the internal audit function. That department, along with all others in the company, had long since become temporary stopping points in the company's executive training program.

After brief stints, perhaps eighteen months, employees move on to their next departmental assignment to prepare the future executive function of the company with the diversity and breadth of experience they'll need to run it. This is a good example of the need to balance competing constraints. The company needs a solid plan to adapt to increasing specialization while still developing future executive breadth of experience.

So, at a minimum, we know that the development of an internal audit director isn't possible. The labor leverage of that director is zero, so our succession choices are limited to hiring from outside the company. And any time succession choices are limited, value management is, by definition, impaired. There are significant costs incurred when intellectual capital is lost through repetitive hiring and development of permanent hires that end up being way less than permanent.

But let's assume first that the company intends to hire the director position. We have two distinct choices. We can hire another traditional internal audit specialist to fill my retiring friend's role. After all, asset conservation and protection is an important and necessary function. But hiring the traditional role, while responsive to cost-and-asset-management needs, doesn't address the growing need for value creation similar to that provided in our earlier example of the shipping-policy consultation.

Hiring an integrative specialist instead of a traditional internal audit department head might not be the correct response either. Our company can't overrespond to allocative efficiency by deciding that the market's demand for value creation trumps asset conservation. The company would be hard-pressed to defend that decision to its external auditors or the US Securities and Exchange Commission (SEC). Having an internal audit function that simply abandons its traditional role of catching bad guys, designing and implementing hard-asset safeguards, and examining expense reports in favor of value management is unacceptable.

While neither of the hiring decisions seems appropriate, the company understands that there's an unrelenting reallocation of resources away from traditional cost-centered functions in accounting (our denominator in the efficiency equation) toward value management (our numerator). They can conceivably hire the traditional skill set and wait until the pressure to respond to allocative efficiency overwhelms them. A lot of companies do exactly that.

One, the Other, or Both?

Then there's the company's choice to contract the internal audit function to one of its accounting firms. Certainly as a small publicly held company, there's obvious single-point-of-failure risk in hiring a department head at all, traditional or integrative, considering that this particular position is the only permanent one in internal audit. So by contracting the position, whatever its makeup, the company can obtain the immediate benefit of not having to worry about the loss of intellectual capital if and when the department head moves on to another job.

This preservation of intellectual capital is at the heart of the traditional rationale for outsourcing the Everything-Else-Department function. When a company takes executive time to manage the scalability—or the growth and contraction—of transactional services and all of the attendant issues, it distracts its relatively more permanent human capital from using its core competencies to create value through creating, selling, producing, and delivering what it has to offer.

Good, Better, Best

The *good* solution to the economy's symbiotic need for value-management scalability companioned with public accounting's growth needs is through providing traditional transactional services like bookkeeping, accounts payable, or payroll services. Clients can buy just the amount they need. This scalability is important to businesses that don't want the risks and managerial burdens of building Everything-Else-Department capability one employee at a time. However, the profitability of providing more commodity services isn't likely up to the standard we've set for ourselves in the Days of the Giants.

A *better* mutually crafted solution is well illustrated by our case-study company as it decides how to replace my friend. If the firm were determining budgetary priorities of that contract, it would be responsible for balancing the allocation of resources between traditional internal auditing and the "decision support" function. As such, it would have experts in both disciplines delivering their particular expertise on a collaborative audit team at the time they were needed.

Our "better" solution is grounded in its ability to move resources between traditional auditing associated with its efficiency *denominator* and integrative auditing of its efficiency *numerator*. Now the accounting firm has something of greater value to offer than it did by just providing scalability of a static set of commodity services, as we see in our "good" solution.

Let's take the analogy a step even further to arrive at our *best* growth plan that offers our client the maximum value-creation capability. Imagine the business leverage we could obtain by achieving the ultimate goal of being the allocator of resources *in and among the numerator services themselves*. Up until now, we've only talked about being grudgingly responsive to allocative efficiency in the economy. Now we can talk about seizing it as the rocket fuel needed by your clients' decision-support function and, not surprisingly, the rocket fuel needed for your firm's growth.

In our role as traditional internal auditors, we've come to learn in the last quarter century that risks don't remain the same for very long in our world of global markets. Perhaps even more so, our decision-support functions, or opportunities, change even more quickly than our hard-asset exposures do. The ability to continually reprioritize risks and opportunities and then address them substantively is something a specialist-led department-of-one is wholly inadequate to manage.

But it *is* entirely within the capabilities of a well-organized, well-resourced, and committed accounting firm. And the truly astounding by-product of the arrangement is that—in solving the value-management crisis for business—we effectively solve our own. We now have internal auditors, consultants, and technicians of all stripes available for value-creation duties.

Instead of being isolated in their respective procedural worlds, they work together to pursue the mission of engagement, transparency, relevance, and choices in their clients' offices. The interdisciplinary relevance problem that plagued us with low practitioner commitment is held at bay. And we can now much more effectively compete for specialist labor in the marketplace.

Mourning the Minders' Demise

It's more than a little sad that we can no longer achieve the relevance to one another with the same tools and methods that we did during the Days of the Giants. They were fun days, slinging resources around, patching things together with our client representatives, and building abiding relationships along the way. But that place—that simpler battleground upon which we created value and bound ourselves together in common purpose—is now being abandoned by the world economy.

Sadly, we won't ever again have the luxury of performing repetitive sets of commodity services in a stable regulatory environment for premium prices as we did in the Days of the Giants. Those Giants had "relationship managers," or Minders, who managed the expectations of a stable popula-tion of buyers. And they had the ad hoc value-creation skills needed to coax maximum value out of cheap year-end services that were funded by a cheap, inexhaustible labor supply.

Our New Giants will not have the luxury of commanding those resources ever again. Their Integrators, the Minders' replacement, will need decision algorithms—grounded in best practices developed in vertical and horizontal lean mechanisms—to create value in the face of fewer and more specialized resources. And they will arrive each successive year, unlike our Giants, to negotiate fees with an even less permanent and increasingly value-hungry population of buyers.

From Theory to Practice

It's fairly easy to sit and ponder the future in what appears to be theoretical terms. What's a little harder to envision, though, are the people and processes that will be required to manage in such an environment. Recommitting to increasing value-creation capability will mean potential havoc for our linear production systems.

As we move into the terrifying world of a *shrinking* body of people taking responsibility for integrating an *expanding* set of competencies, how on earth can we be expected to schedule our work? How will specialist expertise be maintained while we expand toward variable outcomes that customers demand? Who will make decisions about priorities? Isn't this asking for a politically and operationally impossible work environment? Don't we have enough accountability problems already?

We can easily find a professional work environment that's even more complex, interconnected, and under even greater pressure to produce outcomes while abandoning procedure-based value in their work: the practice of medicine. Certainly, in a general way, we can see that our new Integrators will need to behave more like good family-practice physicians. We can see that their decisions about resource application are going to be less and less about unique interpersonal relationships, like a Minder Giant's decisions might have been, and more about applying best-practices algorithms to evidence of business health.

It sounds impersonal—and strikingly similar to the fears that we had in the 1980s about losing our relationship with our family doctors to the big, bad HMO. But in the same manner, and for the exact same reasons, the competing constraints in the economy will soon be taking us there at an accelerated pace.

We can certainly choose to throw up our hands and declare the future to be unattainable today and try to pretend that a simple, direct solution will reveal itself at some future date. As good convergent problem solvers, we have a natural talent for formulating equations with single variables and then aggressively solving for that one variable. Unfortunately, the economy's competing constraints will never again present themselves to us in a way that will allow for such simple, straightforward linear planning.

Design thinking, on the other hand, is a solution-framing process in use today that helps solve complex design problems. It helps not because it's disconnected from reality, but because large, complex, and interconnected systems contain far too many variables to create a linear problem-solving exercise. The problems brought about by large numbers of competing constraints are simply too complex to be solved. They can only be optimized, as we see in medicine today.

But if your firm has (1) made the "big three" market commitments needed to lay the cultural foundation for value-management practice and (2) installed vertical and horizontal lean mechanisms to guide product development and client-service patterns, then you're now ready to start building your new value-management capabilities. Without any one of those preparatory steps, you would not even be in a position to start.

The people, the skills, the processes, and the teams are all waiting for you to discover them. You can then begin to more effectively pursue a professional mission of providing more services to more people, more valuably, and at a declining cost by providing transparency of relevant information so that clients and stakeholders can make choices.

If you've faithfully prepared your firm with the cultural and lean initiatives in our implementation guide so far, you've already completed your hardest work. Your cooperating specialists will do the rest of the work. All you have to do is organize them, inspire them to the goal, and let clinical governance guide them to their cooperating-specialist entrepreneurial destiny.

In doing so, our profession will become the natural repository of an expanding piece of the value-management infrastructure used by the world economy to create, sustain, and enhance value.

And the payoff to your firm and its practitioners will be big.

Chapter 8

Entrepreneurialism by Design

One of the most worrisome trends for our Giants as they try to mentor young practitioners is the perceived lack of entrepreneurial spirit within the next generation. There doesn't seem to be that same drive that people need to find new things to do, crack new markets, and lead others into battle on a new frontier. Since we replaced our departing Finder Giants with salespeople, we've let the upcoming practitioners off the hook to some degree—first in exasperation, then in resignation. Better to leave selling to professionals, we finally conceded.

Of course, we now know that Finders-for-salespeople was not an equal trade. The Finders gave us entrepreneurial spirit. They gave us the ability to grow value through expanding deliverables that our Minders could use to create unlimited outcomes for clients. On the other hand, instead of uncovering unique customer needs, salespeople brought us efficient sales capability for what we had to sell. Now that we've thought about it more carefully, we know that these are not the same things.

And we also know that letting our practitioners, individually and as a group, off the hook for bringing entrepreneurialism to our firms has had the negative effect of disconnecting them from one another. They've lost relevance to one another as complementary value-creation teammates and thus lost a lot of their previous ability to create value together. Now, their relevance to one another is as fellow procedural specialists or commodity producers.

In the Days of the Giants, we were highly competitive generalists who thought first about our clients' needs and then *competed* with one another to meet them. The goal was to add to your firm's shareholder value by building your own competitive "anthill," the sum total of which amounted to the value of your firm. Those anthills were, in effect, traded through an informal bartering system in and among Finders, Minders, and Grinders.

Conversely, and necessarily, in the Days of the New Giants we've bred highly competent specialists who think first about the procedural quality of their specialist work. And, not surprisingly, rather than compete with one another, they *cooperate* to achieve that quality. None of them has an anthill any longer.

We know now that the competitive, individual anthill approach to firms' growth in the age of specialization works against our ability to manage value, or our ability to create value and provide for the succession of that capability. If you think about it, the last thing you want is the value-creation capability you rely on to support shareholder value in the hands of competitive, individual, and apparently irreplaceable entrepreneurs.

From a big-picture perspective, then, it's apparent that we *must* restore entrepreneurialism to our firms to restore our value-creation capability. We cannot let our CPA practitioners off the hook any longer. But restoring the individual entrepreneurialism of competing generalists from the Days of the Giants won't be possible or even desirable. To adapt to the commoditization effect caused by specialization, our new firm-based entrepreneurialism must be built around cooperating specialists. As a result, the Days of the New Giants will require a completely redesigned practice approach that maximizes the group effectiveness of the natural abilities of those practitioners.

There is a story that Albert Einstein once observed that everybody is a genius. The story goes on to caution us that if we judge a fish by its ability to climb a tree, it will live its whole life believing that it is stupid. Much of what passes for succession preparation for our new cooperating specialists—our New Giants—amounts to us trying to teach fish to climb trees. And a lot of private muttering about their inability to climb them passes as valid criticism of their ability to succeed us. It should now be apparent that rather than tree-climbing lessons, our firms' succession capabilities would be vastly better served if we instead provided them with water in which they could swim.

Up until this point, we've done a lot of work to prepare ourselves to restore practitioner commitment by building a new value-creation system for our New Giants. First, we made the "big three" commitments to our profession and to the marketplace. In doing so, we laid the cultural foundation that will prepare us to install the two lean initiatives that will monitor and regulate the efficiency equation of our value-creation efforts, both the denominator and the numerator. Those commitments also required us to define our growth needs in terms consistent with our new professional mission, an important tool for motivating our cooperating specialists.

If you've made it this far in the book, it can't have escaped your notice that your practitioners haven't had to do anything yet. Wasn't this supposed to be a book about the succession crisis? Surely there must be some action *they* can take to move the ball forward. Can't we start training them or something? We need a plan!

Yes, you do indeed need a plan. In fact, you'll need lots of plans and training. And I'll start talking about that soon, but before I do, a brief caveat: The system-design process will likely not be one you've experienced before. Your practitioners will require careful handling and secure positioning to proceed. So before you haul off and start the adventure of designing the Days of the New Giants, you'll want to acknowledge and plan for a few realities about the limits and capabilities of human beings.

Think Big, Sort Of

Tim Brown, the CEO of the international consulting firm Ideo and author of the book, *Change by Design,** captured one aspect of the human challenge well in a discussion with the Mayo Clinic's director of the Center for Innovation, Dr. Nicholas LaRusso. Tim fielded a question from the audience about the nature of design: Doesn't one need to have a good understanding of the big picture to effectively start designing smaller parts of a system?

Tim's response surprised me at first. He dismissed the notion that medicine shouldn't proceed with designing and implementing subsystems in a clinical setting without a complete top-level grasp of how an overall system would work. He did acknowledge that earlier in his career he was tempted to believe that was true, because he's a designer. Left to his own devices, he'd happily keep designing until someone told him to stop.

But as he approached the complexity of a professional service environment as integrated as the Mayo Clinic, he now believes that the reality of huge interconnected and morphing systems require design to be a more collaborative, ground-up construction project. The practitioners would have to build it themselves.

---

* Brown, Tim. *Change By Design: How Design Thinking Transforms Organizations and Inspires Innovation.* New York: HarperCollins, 2009.

He recognized, as should we, that real progress in designing and implementing collaborative professional service systems will only be made through voluntary, decentralized, and practitioner-led initiatives. An implementation style that uses grand-style, top-down *vision* will get us nothing in the way of practitioner engagement. Dr. LaRusso tacitly acknowledged that reality by repeating a favorite saying of practitioners at the Mayo Clinic when they plan to innovate: "Think big. Start small. Move fast."

But *thinking big* to a group of talented, fact-oriented, linear-problem-solving practitioners roughly equates to daydreaming. They have jobs to do, and those jobs are demanding both from the degree of expertise required and the amount of time allotted to perform them. Thinking about something outside their immediate procedural expertise—other than to command that extraneous thought banished to the water cooler—is a fool's errand.

All those busy practitioners want to know about the big picture is that their goal is to engage clients by making relevant information transparent so the clients can make better decisions. And they need to believe that the only way they can really accomplish that is by providing more services to more people, more valuably, and at a declining cost. If you plan to spend your time with practitioners painting complex pictures of the future and how they fit in, they'll leave you in the vapor trail of their far more pressing daily practice duties.

Starting small is a crucial step, too, and one that will challenge you. The moment you start tinkering with the practice worlds of specialists, you'll have to satisfy yourself with baby steps. To maximize your progress, you'll need to limit the size of your process initiatives. The bigger you make your process initiatives, the smaller the process steps within those initiatives need to be. Conversely, the smaller you make your overall initiatives, the better the chance that your teams can accomplish major process steps inside of them.

A good example might be in a process initiative designed to align financial services with individual tax preparation practice. Designing handoffs to and from money management and tax preparation sounds like a fairly small initiative. There are only two departments, and thus only two deciders, and getting them to agree on how to more easily move information from one to the other is a fairly mechanical process.

In contrast, a different initiative that integrates those two functions in addition to the estate and gift-tax function to create a more comprehensive, uniformly executable estate-planning process would now involve multiple parties. You're likely to have confusion across multiple departments, fear of client relationship interference, and loss of status and control by the Minder Giants in the tax preparation function. It's a recipe for trying to do big things and ending up doing nothing.

Moving fast should be a by-product of successfully thinking big, sort of, and starting small. If you've laid enough mission-based foundation with your practitioners and you've not taken too large of a process bite in each underlying initiative, you should be able to move very fast. And the sooner you're able to report small-unit successes, the sooner you can get wider, board-level approval to expand the implementation plan for a value-management system capable of producing the Days of the New Giants.

Our Value-Management Model

It's a core value-management principle that when customers have a positive retail service experience, they tend to credit an *individual* for that trusted, warm feeling. We can all relate to that nice bank teller who recognizes us when we drive up to the window or that hardware store guy who knows just what we're looking for every time we walk into the store. I have to admit that when I'm at the bank experiencing that nice feeling, I don't think to myself, "What a great bank!"

No, I tend to think of the bank only when something goes wrong. It's human nature to credit *people* for good experiences and to blame *organizations* for bad ones. This makes it extremely important that we begin planning to implement firm-based entrepreneurialism immediately. If we don't, as our labor force continues to shrink, specialize, and become increasingly mobile, we risk more than failing the new value-management challenge. We also risk the reduced permanence of our labor force being equally reflected in a decreasingly permanent client base.

A very good example of an organization that has risen above this phenomenon is the Mayo Clinic in Rochester, Minnesota. Internationally renowned for its clinical effectiveness, it's the institution you go to for an "unparalleled patient experience." This is quite the reverse of the typical service organization where "people do good things and organizations fail us." At Mayo, the clinic itself receives appropriate recognition for its great performance. People the world over trust it.

It shouldn't escape our notice that an organization with the reputation for quality of care such as the Mayo Clinic has engaged a top design firm to help it become even better than it already is. If anyone could afford the luxury of resting on its laurels waiting for the rest of medicine to catch up, it would be the Mayo Clinic.

The fact that they're applying such resources to system design right now is not accidental. The Great Recession has not just caused a temporary, if large, dip in the business cycle; it has become a defining moment in the move to great leaps in efficiency, with the (value) numerator in the equation leading the way now instead of the (cost) denominator.

So entrepreneurialism-by-design is the new means by which we'll create the value for which our *institutions* will become known. It will also, not surprisingly, be the growth and profitability engine that will carry us to the Days of the New Giants. Getting to that world not only takes design capability, but also cooperating specialist practitioners motivated to cooperate in new ways.

Who's Carrying Whose Water?

But even with all of their desire to escape a painful present, our New Giants will need to believe that the future is a welcome place where they'll be accepted, loved, and appreciated for their unique contribution to your value-management enterprise. Their forebears' history of competing with one another to create value is still in the too recent past for them to easily accept one another as collaborators. Any collaboration is first viewed through the lens of who'll get credit for the business.

Most of our partner metrics systems today measure, and compensate for, our fish-practitioners' tree-climbing ability first and their swimming ability last. So if we have new business-generation metrics that discourage collaboration, we shouldn't be surprised when they resist cooperating with one another.

If we set about to mechanically try to separate them from their book-of-business relationships so that we can build a system of value creation that credits organizations instead of people, we risk introducing serious behavioral problems. Successfully moving them all to a new collaborative scheme will be as much about the management of fear as it is about inspiration to greatness.

A good example of this is contained in the marketing materials for the Mayo Clinic to prospective physicians. Its governing practice ideals are listed as teamwork, collegiality, professionalism, and mutual respect. There's nothing random about this choice of words. All four principles describe successful relationships of practitioners with one another. *The patients aren't even mentioned.* This is true despite the Mayo Clinic's position as a world leader in operating a patient-centered, outcome-focused care system.

In short, the Mayo Clinic recognizes the limitations of its doctors as human beings. These physicians used to be the Giants who made all the patient-care decisions. And they used to be credited with all of the patient-care success. It was a powerful and rewarding place, this Giant-hood, and to now have it suggested that "the team" is getting credit and that decisions are being made by using best-practices algorithms instead of their own intuitive professional judgment could be an unacceptable, status-lowering prospect.

That is why the published *Mayo Clinic Model of Care** lists its principles in the following order: *First*, it emphasizes practitioner-to-practitioner relationships that are necessary as a foundation for their care model (collegiality, cooperation, and staff teamwork). Only *second* does it list practitioner-to-patient ideals (compassion, trust, and respect for the patient, family, and primary physician). *Listed last* are the ideals of timely, efficient assessment and using the latest technology. Most accounting firms that I know would have a list that is *exactly the reverse* of that prioritization!

In the world of CPA practice, those same fears are in play today. A perceived loss of status relative to other practitioners in a team environment presents a very real barrier to collaborative practice. The barriers go back to the Days of the Giants and their competitive generalist practices and the contribution to firm growth through the building of a practice anthill. In those days, one Giant collaborated with ten subordinates to create value. And if any of the ten collaborators didn't like it, they could hit the road. Giants could be prickly at times.

The collaboration being called for today needs to be conducted among equals, not between one Giant and multiple subordinates. So when the remaining Giants look at one another across the table, they wonder who'll be carrying whose water in this new world of collaboration of equals. And that fear can be paralyzing.

Let me give you a quick practice example. I was talking with a construction client about his company contracting with us to replace what used to be a full-time accounting position. As we chatted about his needs, he mentioned a federal law related to funding and its documentation requirements. And he mentioned it several times, so it seemed important and unique.

I'd heard of this particular law—the Davis–Bacon Act of 1931—and knew that compliance testing for it was a component of Circular A-133 auditing, otherwise known as the Single Audit Act of 1984. We had experts in that

---

* *Mayo Clinic Model of Care*. Mayo Foundation for Medical Education and Research, 2002. http://www.mayo.edu/pmts/mc4200-mc4299/mc4270.pdf.

area of auditing in both our nonprofit and governmental auditing groups. I wanted to suggest that maybe we could design a turnkey Davis–Bacon compliance component in the labor component, with a combination of our payroll experts (Davis–Bacon is a prevailing wage law) and our single-audit experts who had audited construction projects and knew about compliance with that law.

But the need of our time-pressured practitioners to govern their own daily decision making is hardwired into that of a competitive Giant. If the consulting practitioner were to prioritize that consultation according to the referring practitioner's request, it would smack of one Giant telling another one what to do and when to do it.

Generally, in a consultation of this kind, you'll get a nice thank-you and a promise that they'll schedule a discussion with you and your client after their clients are taken care of. Prioritizing a Giant's attention is something you can do with a subordinate, but not with a fellow Giant. So now that we're running out of subordinates due to specialization and productivity, we've got a big value-creation problem.

The ultimate question of who's carrying whose water is actually fairly easily solved, mechanically speaking. A part of your clinical design process will be to set care standards and assess all clients according to those standards. You can then use best-practices algorithms implicit in the criteria of those assessments to guide clients through your collaborative system.

But we must have order even though no one is "in charge" any longer. The loss of Giant governance will have to be replaced by clinical governance as the accountability mechanism driving practitioner behavior. And because this clinical governance system has been built by and for our New Giants, they'll abide by it because they're cooperating specialists who want to do the right thing. Always. It's the water our fish-practitioners need to begin swimming in instead of trying to climb trees.

But what we want to absorb at this point in our journey to the Days of the New Giants is clear. Despite the fact that the operation of your collaborative system needs to be patient- and outcome-focused, you should gear most of your marketing toward managing practitioners' fears about loss of status and control in their daily lives, just as Mayo has done.

As we try to motivate practitioners, we might be tempted to make a lot of sideways, flowery, and unattainable value assertions to the marketplace, but this actually *damages* our ability to set the culture they need to achieve that value-producing capability together. They'll need to be continually reminded that they are not in competition with one another, and that best practices aimed at efficient client care dictate that resource allocation be based on all clinic members' needs. And one of those allocated resources is their own time.

You cannot escape this reality, so count on incorporating large doses of the terms *teamwork, collegiality, professionalism,* and *mutual respect* in your design and implementation processes.

With or without Mayo?

So we've concluded that any plan intended to provide enough profitability to sustain a practitioner-owned financial-succession program depends on our future ability to manage value in the face of even greater specialization pressure. We're now faced with our last major decision. The pace and nature of merger and spinoff that we have seen in medicine throughout the last quarter century is now at our door: Our practitioners will similarly have to scramble to find their place in a substantially altered new order.

We should anticipate the coming wave of business combination and creative integration strategy by envisioning, and then deciding, where we fit in that future world before it decides for us. In short, you need to decide if you want to create your own clinic, become a part of someone else's clinic, or simply isolate yourselves as specialty service providers—a sort of "with or without Mayo," if you will.

Accounting firms across the country deliver all sorts of services. Some integrate naturally and easily, and some don't. Some of us have aggressively added ancillary services, and some have abandoned them all in favor of returning to traditional practice of taxation and one or two auditing specialties. There is no wrong answer here.

As a result, the first design consideration that applies to all firms today in their quest to arrive at the Days of the New Giants is to determine what value creation looks like specifically for them. You don't want to be designing value-creation systems for people and services that you don't plan on integrating with one another. Nor do you want to exclude any value-creation potential for which your firm, or a partnering organization, does have the necessary "lumber." We want to have a pretty good idea of where our integration borders are so that we can plan more effective realization.

Your firm's size won't always be the ultimate determinant, but it's fairly clear that the larger your firm is, the more likely it is that it will have enough major infrastructure components onboard to be able to integrate its own infrastructure offerings. Generally, smaller firms will have fewer specialties and will most likely decide to position as specialists.

A good example of disjointed procedural specialist practice is illustrated in my recent need of minor surgery. I hadn't had surgery in some 30 years, so I'd forgotten just how something that seemed to me to be one event could really be five. In the weeks after the procedure I received five separate bills: one each from the surgeon, the anesthesiologist, the anesthetist, the surgery center, and the referring physician.

Each of them had a procedural value, and none of them, save for my long-suffering internist, had an interest in the overall patient experience except to the extent that their own procedure was involved. I fell asleep before surgery and never saw the surgeon again.

I was chatting about this with a colleague from another firm who had some previous experience in dealing with physician compensation. As I described the premise of my work and the foundational analogy of specialist practice in medicine, he exclaimed, "And you'll be paid on an eat-what-you-kill basis!" He presumed at the time that my advocacy of the medical-practice analogy amounted to my promoting that type of a value-creation system in my own work. Of course, the point of value-creation practice is exactly the opposite.

But still, further isolation of your specialist practitioners is a choice you can make with your head held high. There's no shame in becoming the best darned procedural specialist you can be. Just don't expect a lot of business leverage to magically rise up out of the ashes like it did back in the Days of the Giants. The easy value-creation days are over.

The other branch in the decision tree is the choice to build our own value-creation systems complete with plans, lumber, glue, nails, windows, and doors. This is the group of firms that has decided to take matters into their own hands and reconstruct value-creation capability internally to create the Days of the New Giants. These firms are generally large enough to have adequate specialist services to develop significant infrastructure components for their clients. They contain not only the expertise, or the lumber, needed to build the new value-creation systems, but they're also prepared to commit to buying the plans, nails, and glue needed to build a structure capable of creating value in the future.

For this group of firms that are going to position themselves as infrastructure providers, or *value management* enterprises, the design issues are big. While the vastness of product offerings at some accounting firms is something we've historically touted as giving us market power, the reality is that much of that vastness has now become a liability to us.

While adding to the vast sea of specialist silos used to be seen as a leverage opportunity in the pre–Great Recession global economy, it's more accurately exposed now as a lack of focus. Only through integration of those vast services can you expect to compete in the Days of the New Giants.

So regardless of your firm's existing services, some thought about your position in the world of product and service integration is critical *now*.

To Merge or Not to Merge

A lot has been written about accounting firm culture as a primary driver, or limitation, in accounting firm mergers. The discussion is almost always cast as a negotiation for the new political order of Giant governance that will be created. As such, these discussions come nowhere near the real issue of the need to replace Giant governance with clinical governance for our New Giants to manage value in the future.

However, as an industry, we've been successful at transitioning from Giant-led value-creation practice to specialist-led procedural practice. And there's value in that, despite the fact that value management has suffered so terribly. And the benefit is in the fact that our fish-practitioners have resoundingly demonstrated that they're much more effective cooperating with one another, or swimming, than they are in a tree-climbing competition.

This bodes well for practitioner-built and -led value-management systems. Our cooperating specialists will follow their own rules. They just need to build rule sets that respond to the economy's value-management needs. If they do, they'll together become the value-management engine that we and the economy need them to become. If they don't, we can all look forward to endless streams of cooperative-specialist procedures while someone else builds the value-management infrastructure of the Everything-Else Department being demanded by the world economy.

To more easily grasp the importance of specialty integration as we move into the future, think for a moment from the perspective of a consumer of professional services. Imagine you're at the Mayo Clinic the day it suddenly changes from an integrated, patient-focused, value-creation machine to one building that contains all the services it does today, but without the culture and operations of its clinical governance system.

You're greeted at the door by a receptionist, who assures you that the Mayo Clinic has more and better resources than any other clinical system in the world. "Welcome to the Mayo Clinic. Which one of our world-class experts would you like to see today?"

And here you were, foolish enough to believe that *they* were going to tell *you* which experts you should see to help you get better. Silly you.

Chapter 9

Build Your Own Mayo Clinic

The need to move toward clinically delivered, outcome-based results in our profession is the result of the relentless clashing of important market constraints that demand ever more value and ever-growing specialization. We cannot solve one and ignore the other. We must optimize the balance of the two. And organizing our cooperating specialists into a value-creation array is the only way to serve both of those competing masters.

The solving of value-creation capability should be a compelling enough reason to create our own version of the Mayo Clinic in our firms all by itself. But now that we know our *value-management* capabilities—those that contain a built-in succession mechanism—are the real end-game goal for both ourselves and our clients, we're especially interested in organizing clinically as cooperating specialists.

Technology and global communications now afford nearly universal access to the means of production. Increasingly, your practitioners are capable of serving clients in traditional, transactional ways from anywhere in the world. And they're capable of providing those specialist services to clients without the need to be associated with your firm. That prospect gets scarier as one remembers the customer phenomenon: People get credit for creating value, and organizations get blamed for a lack of it.

These realities make institutionally controlled value-creation capability more critical and difficult than ever. So how can we build accounting firms that consistently deliver higher value outputs than is possible for individuals? The model for building a professional-services institution that actually gets credited for its outcome-producing capabilities exists in Rochester, Minnesota, at the Mayo Clinic.

Despite the fact that "thinking big" is a necessary first step as accounting firms attempt to build our own Mayo Clinics, we know we need to "start small" and "move fast" to begin. The breadth of the picture we paint while we're thinking big should always be tempered by the reality that people's daily work lives will be significantly affected as we implement the Days of the New Giants. And those hardworking folks may be affected negatively for some time before positive results come. All of us will need the zeal made possible by our new mission to fight our way through those challenging moments together.

The remainder of this book describes the building blocks of that big picture. In doing so, it tries to describe those building blocks in an accessible way for CPA practitioners, not process experts. It should serve as an implementation manual that you can use to help you fulfill the mission of your firms, and its practitioners, in increasingly rewarding ways. In its simplest terms, a clinical environment comprises the following four things:

- Standards of care
- Algorithms
- People
- Processes

From Giants to Standards of Care

Clinical governance is a term made popular in the mid-1990s to describe how care standards are enforced in medicine. In our case now, too, we realize we can no longer have our Giants enforce their own care standards. Resources are too expensive and specialized these days, and complex outcomes are almost impossible to achieve cost effectively unless we have a way to bring order to our practitioner groups.

Over the course of the last decade or so, we've enforced order by building linear production schemes for our core products of financial statements and tax returns, thus creating care standards for specific procedures. Clinical governance will now be the mechanism that allows us to integrate those individual departmental procedural standards into a larger, outcome-producing set of care standards covering primary care for our clients' Everything-Else Departments—a much bigger and more profitable target.

Clinical governance, always tempered by professional judgment, describes the replacement of the Giants' governance by barking orders to cheap, plentiful, and generally skilled labor. Similarly, our primary clinical care standards—founded in consumer perception of value—do not *replace* but *integrate* the individual specialist care standards of the New Giants into the larger clinical mission.

Successful replacement of our departing Giants' individual value-creation standards and methods with clinical care standards and methods based on our clients' needs will mean that we can some day decommission our vertical and horizontal lean teams. As we're able to bring our customers into our new clinic under these new primary-care standards, we'll rarely need to, in effect, "fix" our processes by picking off non-value-added costs. Neither will we need to fix our horizontal integration capabilities in client service patterns. They will already have been optimized by faithful execution of those standards starting from the moment a client arrives at your clinic.

Algorithms

Practice algorithms are the decision engines we'll need in our new environment of collaborating specialists. As you might imagine, those decision mechanisms must be designed to originate directly from, and be responsive to, our standards of care. From the very first point of entry into our clinical environments, our clients must feel that there's a larger goal our firms are working toward than the specific procedure (usually a tax return or financial statement) that brought them to you in the first place.

And we need algorithms to reduce chaos in our clinics. As we continue to decommission our Giants, we're left with fewer practitioners to bark value-creation orders to our troops. Not surprisingly, there are far fewer troops waiting around to take those orders. So, if we expect to operate smoothly, we'll need decision mechanisms that tell collaborating specialists—previously unaccustomed to taking direction from anyone—what actions to take for our firms to achieve the highest likelihood of positive outcomes.

Up until now, our response to the chaos created by competing Giants has been to restrict their movements within a shrunken universe of deliverables by providing them with simplified, linear standards of care aimed at commoditizing their specialist procedures. While turning our competing Giants into cooperating specialists helped solve the chaos problem, it also had the unfortunate side effect of "solving" our value-creation capabilities with it. To reverse that side effect, we need to install clinical decision-making tools derived from our clients' perceptions of their own needs so that, more than just procedures, value itself can be created in a rational, executable, and efficient fashion.

In Chapter 10, we'll talk further about algorithms, where they come from, and what they can do for us and our clients.

People

The good news is that we already have most of the people we need to create the Days of the New Giants. However, there's one conspicuously missing specialist: the new Minder. The training of the replacement for Minder Giants and their introduction to groups of collaborating specialists will be one of the most critical things you'll do in building your new clinical system.

The Vision Project of the American Institute of Certified Public Accountants (AICPA) tacitly acknowledges the need for this new specialty in its statement about core competencies as a relevant consideration in projecting training needs. Interestingly, one of the project's assertions is that the concept of establishing core competencies in our profession is gradually becoming *less relevant*. The rationale for this is contained in the explosion of CPA specialization and related support systems. There's just too much going on to make core competencies useful as a concept.

I suspect that medicine could have made the same assertion a hundred years ago. "There's just too much going on for us to describe it concisely and plan to build it all into one person," they could have lamented. And they would have been right. But the Mayos' conclusion at that time was not to throw up their hands in concession to the specialization constraint, but to declare that, as generalization declined, there needed to be a counterbalancing rise in the core competency of integration.

Chapter 11 addresses the need for integration specialists and the necessary training and core competencies of that service capability.

Processes

We're no longer strangers to process. We've already learned an appreciation for uniformity and have been enforcing limited care standards related to a couple of our traditional products for quite a while now. We generally refer to these standards as our "paperless" production systems, and they serve as the backbone of the majority of the revenue streams that keep most of us in business.

Unfortunately, though, by elevating our standards of care for tax return production, for example, we've actually lowered our primary-care standards for a good piece of the value-creation opportunity we used to enjoy in the Days of the Giants. The key misunderstanding we've labored under in our process initiatives up until now is to mistake *uniformity* to mean *linearity*. They're not the same thing.

Processes can be *uniformly nonlinear*, allowing decision branches through the use of practice algorithms that recognize that not all of our clients come to us in the same condition. The ability to produce outcomes instead of mere procedures will actually *require* that we use nonlinear uniform processes to cope better with trying to use our highly specialized labor (or "increasingly variable inputs" in process language) to create positive outcomes (or "variable outputs," as our process friends would say).

Primary-care clinical processes will require assessment, diagnosis, outcome identification, planning, implementation, and evaluation for a still well-defined but considerably expanded universe of conditions common in our clients' Everything-Else Departments. Without those processes, our procedural specialists will continue to zoom right past all of that opportunity to create value, instead spending all of their resources training the guns of production on our traditional busy-season battlefield—that place that the global economy is now leaving.

In Chapter 12, we'll talk about process uniformity vs. linearity, our value-creation processes, and the teams that will lead primary-care services in support of our specialists.

Status and Professionalism

Historically, our Giants operated in hierarchical systems not unlike those of the medical profession of a half century ago. They got to make any decisions they felt inclined to make and to accept or ignore the input of others of equal or lower status without consequence. It was a powerful place to be, this Giant-hood, and having risen to the top of such a system certainly had its benefits.

So whenever Giants think you might be attacking their status, you'll have a serious leadership problem. They'll deploy all of their worst Giant behaviors in resistance to you. And they'll do this *despite* the fact that they might feel frustrated and unsuccessful under the combined yoke of internal administrative paper shuffling, unrealistic customer demands, and what appears to be increasingly willful and uncooperative junior colleagues. That potential loss of status will feel like the last straw.

Process redesign that proposes to flatten a Giant's system into a collaborative structure sounds to them like a kick in the pants. And if they believe that to be true, your clinic-building days will be short-lived. Dr. Nicholas LaRusso acknowledged this in his presentation with Ideo's Tim Brown* on interactions between Mayo doctors and Ideo's design engineers. Dr. LaRusso conceded that the discussions between the design engineers and the physicians started unproductively and didn't improve until everyone understood their roles.

Reading between the lines, you could paraphrase the conclusion of the previous sentence to "until everyone made sure that their status would not be lowered in the process." I'm guessing the practitioners' initial fears were that their professional decision making would now be subject to review by, or somehow subordinate to, design engineers.

Thus, the first task in your clinic-building scheme needs to be to have those status-assuring discussions with the New Giants. Without them, Giants listening to your big ideas will be preoccupied—not with the complexity of a new practice system, which is distracting enough, but with projecting their position, or status, outward into this brave new world of value management.

So before we haul off and talk with our practitioners about the power they'll lose, let's paint the picture of power and status they'll gain. Traditionally, in the Days of the Giants, our status map looked like the one shown in Figure 9.1.

The typical labor-leverage scheme started with our Finders, who obtained work. Their status was unquestioned, and ultimately they needed to be answered to by the Minders and Grinders, who were delivering on the Finders' promises. The need for the Giants' system was rooted not in any inherent Machiavellian tradition of accountants, but in the real needs of the value-creation system. When we promised something, we damned well had better deliver it. So the Giants' political pecking order served the very practical and valuable function of a feedback loop that ensured performance of work and achievement of outcome at the level the Finders had promised our clients.

But the leadership residue left behind from those days lingers today. During my second attempt at research for this work, I interviewed some of the next generation of political leadership in public accounting as well as

---

* Brown, Tim. *Change by Design: How Design Thinking Transforms Organizations and Inspires Innovation*. New York: HarperCollins, 2009.

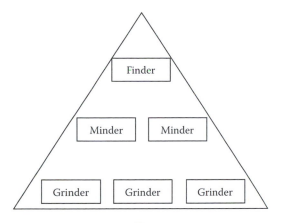

Figure 9.1   Status map of the Giants.

their advisers. After discussions about what was going on and what should be done about it, I wanted to be sure I didn't leave any meeting without getting to the core of the spirit of how they perceived the weight of their new ascendancy to power. Did they have any particular sense of mission that differed from their departing retirees? How did they feel about the future?

Universally, their emotional response could be summed up with a four-word sentence: "It's my turn now." Despite the fact that the value-creation pyramids of the past effectively ensured firm growth through value creation, including the feedback loop that we're missing so badly right now in the absence of the Finders, the emotional release of their now being freed from the servitude of retiring Giants was palpable.

So we know that we need to account for maintaining or elevating the status of our specialist practitioners in our new clinical arrangement. We know that we need to provide them with our Chapter 4 client-centered professional mission to save them the disappointment of not getting to act like the Giants of old in this new value-creation universe. At this critical juncture of our profession, "Now, I get to be the Giant" is decidedly not the leadership tenor you want in your partner group individually or as a partner culture.

But to suggest that, right at the point of their acquisition of a firm's political power, the Finders and Minders will be replaced by a new set of Giants—called salespeople and integrators, to whom they must report and be subservient—will be unacceptable to them. People first need to understand their roles, just as the Mayo doctors and their supporting design engineers did.

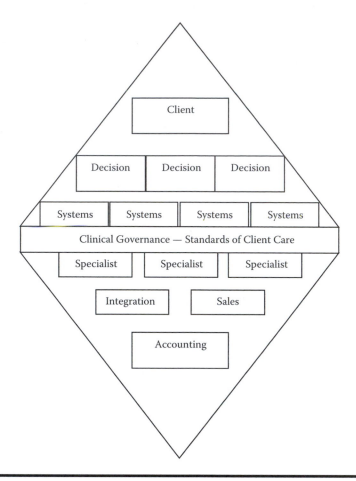

Figure 9.2 Status map of the clinic.

As the graphic in Figure 9.2 demonstrates, the sales and integration functions are not higher status positions than the specialist practitioners in the
way that the Finders and Minders dominated the Grinders. They're actually good-servant positions designed to assist our New Giants in realizing
the highest standard of primary care possible. They're not a labor-leverage
system overlaying a feedback loop that supports an effective, but horribly
inefficient, value-creation system like our departing Giants had.

The reality of professional practice that is capable of producing outcomes
is that no one gets to be in charge of our practitioners' lives. Unlike our
departing Giants, *collaborating specialists are subservient to no other practitioners* in their value-creation universe. Instead, they're duty-bound by the firm's
care standards *in both primary and specialty care.* This is an important collaborative migration that eliminates practitioner-on-practitioner subservience,

a source of irritation for our New Giants, and replaces it with a duty to the highest level of clinical performance, a source of missionary pride.

The interface between you and your clinic's clients will now be governed by its standards of care rather than by the dictates of Giants. While this is already true today to a large degree, the big difference in our new practice approach is that now we'll plan to lead with our *primary-care* standards rather than leading with our *specialty-care* ones. It's the same discipline you employ today in your paperless production systems but with an expanded rule set.

A good example of this smoother clinical operation and resulting higher performance without status loss is illustrated in Chapter 8, where we attempt to design a piece of cross-functional infrastructure in a client's office. You'll recall that we needed an audit specialist with Circular A-133 Single Audit experience, a payroll specialist (generally of much lower status in the traditional pecking order), and the client service partner (a tax partner with construction expertise). The goal was to embed a compliance component for the Davis–Bacon Act of 1934 (a prevailing-wage law) into a payroll offering of the firm for our construction-management client.

Not coincidentally, the audit and tax specialists in our example happened to be from the exact two departments I cited back in Chapter 2—departments that, as my colleague said, "could be in separate buildings." His statement alluded to the limited cross-functional contact that had historically occurred.

Typically, in this type of a scenario of low connectedness among departmental "silos" and one collaborating member from a low-status function (payroll), the best you could hope for from the audit specialist was one of the following:

- That he wasn't busy (never true except when he was on vacation)
- That he owed you a quid-pro-quo favor from a previous transaction (almost never true, because the departments have no production history that would generate such a transaction)
- That he was subordinate or otherwise politically beholden to someone who *did* owe you that favor (a completely random chance)

In the Days of the New Giants, we won't have the luxury of using informal political negotiation of individual Giant-determined standards of care. The most important reason we need client-centered primary-care standards among specialists is to enforce professionalism. For example, assume for a moment in our example that our audit specialist was not inclined to join the problem-solving effort of helping to build the aforementioned piece of compliance infrastructure.

In our past world of *competing Giants*, the Finder of this work would have asked a Minder to look into the possibility of providing such a service. The Minder would have had access to plenty of Grinders to look up the Davis–Bacon Act requirements and figure out a way to get the job done. Seniority, complementary value-creation skills, and a built-in feedback loop were all neatly tied up in one package.

Today, in our transitional world of *competing specialists*, the response would be, "Sorry. I'd love to help, but I'm too busy right now. Call me after the busy season." The first partner asked for what amounted to a personal favor and was politely, but firmly, turned down. There's no Finder/Minder relationship to enforce the consultation; the value-creation skills between the two partners are not complementary (although the professional subject matter is); and the consultation dies on the vine. And we hardly need a feedback loop if we aren't bothering to create excess value in the first place. Here we have a completely broken value-creation function.

Now let's project ourselves to our inevitable future, which is in the practice of *cooperating specialists*. In this world, our firm is committed to expanding outcomes but needs to do so in an orderly manner. Because of this, we've introduced a practice algorithm originating from our firm's primary-care standards that requires requests for infrastructure assessment to be responded to within two weeks.

Now, the first partner is not making a personal request requiring political connection to be successful, but rather is initiating a professional consultation coded into your firm's standards of care. Our second partner's negative response would now not be the polite declining of a personal favor, but a serious professional lapse. In effect, the response would be, "Sorry, but I'm too busy right now to abide by our firm's primary-care standards." Assuming your practitioners negotiated those underlying care standards, they will abide by the resulting rules without question. Your cooperating specialists will do the right thing. Always.

A good way for your practitioners to think about this, without mourning too loudly the loss of power of the Giants, is in the following widely understood governance analogy.

We the Practitioners

We can think of our commitment to *clinical governance* as our constitution itself. Our constitution establishes the rule of law. It defines us less as to what we do as practitioners than it does as to *who we are*. It cannot only serve as a way to accept some loss of power and autonomy; it must also serve to elevate that inevitable loss of individual prerogative as serving an exalted moral purpose, just as the US Constitution does for us as a nation.

The commitment to the rule of law contained in our clinical governance provisions would be incomplete without the actual laws themselves. These are our *standards of care*. While we have been very good at building laws founded in specialty-care standards for a few products and services (tax returns and audits), we've been woefully inadequate in passing laws that govern primary care.

And this has made it impossible for our firms to profitably penetrate beyond the specialty services, or commodity, level of our clients' infrastructures into the decision-support level, where value in excess of the sum of all commodity services resides.

And I know my fellow practitioners will understand the need for regulations and other administrative laws that clarify or expand a legislative body of law. Our clinical practice's administrative law is contained in *algorithms* that help us make the decisions of day-to-day practice. We need them to have any hope of providing more services to more people, more valuably, and at a declining cost in an organized, executable, and increasingly valuable way.

The Journey so Far

Our success at organizing cooperating specialists into a value-creation array in our clinics will depend on how carefully we've assembled the cultural and process building blocks we've talked about so far.

First, we needed practitioners focused, as a group, on their mission of serving the decision-support needs of our clients and all of their stakeholders. We made the "big three" market commitments knowing we needed to do so to solve our practitioner-to-practitioner commitment deficit, which was preventing us from achieving group focus.

Profitability needs dictate that we move into the realm of the Days of the New Giants without incurring additional costs. We no longer have extra cash to throw away, so we know that vertical and horizontal cost and value initiatives are going to be critical to monitoring both the numerator and the denominator of our efficiency equations. We must find a way to pay for building our new clinical environments as we go.

And then we had a decision to make about whether to remain strictly procedural specialists or commit to building our own clinical value-management enterprises. "With or without Mayo" is a key decision for our boards to make. Any discussion of your firm's "value proposition" that fails to recognize the need to manage the balance of outcomes with specialization should be looked at very critically. Your firm's strategy is not a marketing exercise, and there isn't time to pretend any longer about our firms' value-management prospects.

If, after all these barriers are overcome, we've decided to proceed with leading the creation of the Days of the New Giants, we know we need to have order. As our original Giants disappear into history, we'll have lost our last few value-creation order givers. In response, we will need to (1) constitute ourselves as a governing body and (2) build rules and regulations governing our new client-centered care standards so we can deliver value as a practitioner group.

Value-management capability will not magically rise up out of the ashes of self-interest as it did in the competitive-generalist Days of the Giants. The future can be a rewarding problem-solving adventure, or it can continue as a procedure-producing death march, depending on the following:

- The sincerity of your cultural commitments
- The quality of your efficiency efforts and metrics
- The constitutional strength of your clinical governance.

As the ownership structures of our firms flatten in response to the specialization constraint, it's critical that our partner groups now be united by something more compelling than "It's my turn now."

Chapter 10

The Decision Engines

The power to make decisions is, well, empowering. If you give employees the leeway to make their own decisions in pursuit of job performance standards, they'll be more likely to take responsibility for meeting them. And if there are standards to which they didn't quite measure up the first time, they'll be more likely to renew their commitment for each successive try if they have input in deciding what means to employ in those efforts.

The need for practice algorithms now to build outcome-producing capabilities in our accounting firms runs counter to this intuitive understanding of employee motivation. We want practitioners more motivated than ever to engage one another in value-creation pursuits. In the past, that ability to make independent decisions and apply resources at will was the very source of our Giantness. To think now that it might be one of the things we need to give up to build a value-management enterprise is, at best, unsettling.

But while it's true that the specter of interference in our decision making threatens our feelings of professional status and power, we've already voluntarily begun the process of letting go. In the Days of the Giants, we were able to stop processes midstream to divert our attention away from compliance work to get answers to client questions or engage in problem-solving services. We even *looked for* those client problems—sometimes right during engagements—and Giants were free to engage in their own process inventions. At the whim of any particular Giant, resources could be quickly reallocated and applied to whatever client problem arose.

But since those days, the loss of our Finder Giants and the imminent extinction of our Minders and our need to produce ever more tax returns and audits in an ever smaller time allotment has gradually led to fewer and fewer choices for ourselves and, unfortunately, for our clients. That choice to limit our own process options was taken voluntarily, and even willingly, because it was for the good of the team. This is an important leadership point as we look for ways to ask our practitioners, for the good of the team, to voluntarily limit their own choices in deference to those of our clients.

Uniformity vs. Linearity

The original hope for process development in accounting firms was that it would be the great efficiency savior. We even gave our efforts the sustainability-sounding nickname "paperless" to give it a "green" feel, which made for great internal marketing, too. What this evolutionary step taught us was that professionals will cooperate with one another. They'll even willingly restrict their individual choice making in the pursuit of a common goal that they believe serves everyone equally and ensures the highest procedural quality. Our cooperating specialists always want to do the right thing.

Unfortunately, along the way, we cooperated so well internally, converging ultimately on the goal of strictly uniform procedural systems, that we eventually arrived at the place where our practice algorithms looked a lot like telephone poles. They were straight as a stick, with our only choice being to move a project forward to the next production station or move it backward to the previous station for rework.

Added to our increased internal orderliness, our client communications increasingly became about how they could constrain their information systems and conform their daily activities to ours for the sake of our internal production schemes. As a result, our communications with them were less about their needs (our primary-care efficiency numerator) and more about our processes (our specialist-care efficiency denominator). We eventually realized that our fundamental error was to have mistaken process *linearity* for process *uniformity*.

What we're becoming painfully aware of now in our new era of a value-conscious market is that our cooperating specialists need primary-care practice decision-making tools that, along with our uniformly linear specialist procedural algorithms, are uniformly responsive to client needs, or *uniformly nonlinear.* This reality will present us with far more difficult practice-design problems than our specialist paperless production systems ever did. And that's because the design goal will be to allow the highest degree of outcome-measured success, or output variability, at the lowest costs of production in serving our clients instead of simply being concerned solely with lowest cost specialist procedures.

And now, once again, our specialists will have the opportunity to voluntarily conform their decision making to clinical governance standards, for the greater good of everyone, in a manner and for reasons much like their voluntary restriction of choice as they developed their paperless production systems. Remember, our cooperating specialists always want to do the right thing.

So Where Do We Start?

If we look back to the reasons we developed practice algorithms in the last ten years in our paperless production systems, we can find good guidance on the design of new ones. As we developed algorithms founded in our specialist standards of care, we were guided by much the same motivation as we are today in needing to develop expanded primary-care algorithms. Standardized decision making was intended to reduce errors, provide for seamless specialist practitioner replacement, and improve adherence to procedural best practices—all laudable goals that need to remain in our work.

What's new today as we design and implement our primary-care standards is not that we need to replace those algorithms. Rather, we need to augment them with group decision-making mechanisms that equip people with the tools they'll need to describe, solve, and plan for treating complex problems that can involve many previously disconnected specialists. And we need to be able to accomplish this recognizing that we don't have access to cheap and unlimited labor sources like we did in the Days of the Giants.

Although the fundamental practice mechanisms of assessment, planning, and execution still apply just as they do now in our specialist procedural mills, value-management practice will require clear differences in just what is being assessed. And there will be major differences in executing action plans not for hordes of hierarchically led cheap labor, but for a flat array of expensive collaborating specialists—a much different proposition.

Properly designed and executed, those decision engines will be very effective at coordinating our specialists into a value-creation array. But to construct those engines, we need to first imagine just what it is we want to accomplish for our clients. We need to be able to describe their condition as they come to us for engagement, and then make a plan to help them get to their best outcome-based results. Fortunately, you'll already have had lots of practice at this during your Chapter 6 horizontal lean work.

Having worked through the assessment of the general health, cost-effectiveness, and scalability of each major client's Everything-Else-Department infrastructure, you'll be well prepared to make this assessment now for incoming client relationships. This will have you better prepared to execute a wider clinical approach from the very start of your client engagements.

Assessment

In our current world of high-quality, but commoditized, specialist-care procedures, we already begin every engagement by assessing our client's condition, but only in a very small way. For example, in most production systems I know, the assessment of client condition is something like "unaudited" or "tax return-less" before our procedures begin. And our expected outcome is something like "audited" or "tax return-ful." This certainly simplifies, and makes linear, the process of what we do in between assessment and completion, but it does little to address the greater health and well-being of our clients' Everything-Else Departments.

So it makes sense that if we want to expand our clinics' outcome-producing potential, we need to start our assessment process from a much larger and more general business-infrastructure-health starting point. Our specialist procedures, like tax returns and audits, will undoubtedly continue to be relatively linear once we get to them, but we need to start our Everything-Else-Department assessment process from a top-level quality standpoint for a couple of very good reasons.

First, and most obvious, if our assessment and work program for each client starts from the premise of either "unaudited" or "tax return-less," we'll be restricting ourselves to just that procedure. In the Days of the Giants, we had Finders and Minders sniffing around the offices of buyers in our clients' offices during engagement performance. Those Giants are close to extinction now, and the specialists working on each engagement are very busy concentrating in their specialist areas and producing chargeable time.

If we want to reverse that negative value-creation trend and turn ourselves, together, into a value-management engine, we can no longer allow such a limited specialty-care assessment to lead our engagement processes. If we expect to become the developers, growers, and protectors of the relevance, transparency, and choices infrastructures of our clients' Everything-Else Departments, we'll need a practice methodology that will allow our specialists to perform together as a team in that role.

But perhaps even more important to our specialists, I suspect that sometimes the lack of transparency, relevance, and choices in the tax and financial reporting functions of our clients' offices is actually a contributor to their own misery during busy seasons. The opportunity then is not just to continually expand an economic relationship with clients for the tawdry sake of "making more money," but to become a sustaining contributor to the value-management capabilities of their clients' Everything-Else Departments. And the tax and financial reporting mechanisms are an important part of that infrastructure that can both provide more value to the enterprise *and* make your busy-season lives better as a by-product.

Unfortunately, we historically accepted these weaknesses and engaged in sometimes massive amounts of rework and deferred transactional analysis, accessing and coordinating the patchwork information systems of our clients. And we did this all for the privilege of having the year-end work. But now that allocative efficiency has permanently removed a large percentage of resources from year-end activities, we simply don't have the funds as an economy to operate that way any longer.

Along with that sobering reality, the twin (and inversely related) arcs of the decline of the Giants value-creation systems and the accelerating cost of our specialist labor have combined to produce a price–value tipping point. Our billing rates have now become fundamentally, and permanently, irrelevant to the economy.

As a result, it has become critical that we begin delivering even our core products more valuably as a necessary and unavoidable first step of developing the capacity to deliver all other Everything-Else-Department infrastructure more valuably. Fortunately, now that we know we have a fixable practice-design problem, we have exactly the people who can fix it. With a little guidance, our cooperating specialists will do the right thing. Always.

Learn by Doing

Our Chapter 6 horizontal lean example was a case study where we took charitable organization audit and tax engagements and—working backward from a painful lack of value-creation practice—recast our client's Everything-Else Department. We did so through an infrastructure assessment process that led to the potential of tripling our client revenue while reducing practitioner busy-season work by 75 percent. The client was put in a position to win, too, reducing the overall cost of his organizations' process infrastructure by over 20 percent.

While this was a nice proposed result, it could only come to light after our client had suffered terribly with us. He'd unwittingly failed to follow important tax regulations and unintentionally run afoul of audit requirements all year long while we either recovered from our previous busy season or performed pressing specialist procedural work for other clients.

This client's Everything-Else Department was underperforming horribly, but our specialist assessment and action plan gave us no way to respond other than to:

- Observe their failures after the end of the year
- Punish them for underperforming with negative tax and audit consequences
- Fail to effectively arm them with structural solutions to the causes of those failures

We accomplished pretty much the opposite of relevance, transparency, and choices—our newly urgent professional mission.

The assessment processes that our firms will be building now, and the resulting evidence-based primary-care algorithm-driven practice execution, will not be uniform across our profession in the near term. Yours won't need to look like those of any other clinic. In fact, the reality is that they'll necessarily look different because of variations in the combinations of your firm's available clinical services.

Some of your firms will have financial services, technology, human capital, labor-outsourcing systems, and other ancillary service components that contribute to the value-management function of the Everything-Else Department. Some firms may be strictly audit and tax specialty shops that are partnering with outside infrastructure providers to address value management.

But the common goal of the design and operation of all our practice systems must be first to address building our value-creation capability and then to devise non-labor-dependent succession of that capability to properly serve the needs of our value-conscious economy. We can either do that or make plans to settle for permanently reduced business leverage as a new fact of life.

Deja Vu, Revisited

If there's one thing we departing Giants will remember (and will never fail to proudly retell you with little or no prompting), it's that in our prime we were great problem solvers and mistake fixers. Whatever our clients' transactional work produced, we'd analyze it and make a few journal entries, pushing all of the mistakes out of the balance sheet. We'd then arrive at a set of financial statements that were a pretty good representation of the earnings, financial position, and funds flow. Fixing stuff after the fact was one of our best skills.

Now, one last time, all of the skills we developed in devising analytical workarounds to make up for a poorly designed and executed transactional system can assist us with the design of our new value-management systems. Sometimes the most effective approach to designing something that will work well is to reverse-engineer something that didn't.

In our Chapter 6 horizontal lean case study, our nonprofit organizations found their way back to a proposed Everything-Else-Department infrastructure that significantly improved transparency, relevance, and choices. And they did so with a proposed cost reduction of more than 20 percent. This case had all the hallmarks of excessive non-value-added costs, poorly designed and executed transactional work, nonintegrated services, and technology that impaired relevance and transparency. It made intelligent compliance choices impossible.

So what if, instead of entering the previous busy seasons with an assessment of "unaudited and tax return-less," we would have first had a primary-care assessment as the basis for starting our services for the year? What would that look like? If our decision making would possibly involve a number of specialists, what would be the basis for referral? Who'd be in charge? It sounds like things could get very messy in a hurry without a rational, coordinated plan.

But we know from our Chapter 9 clinical-governance discussion that a nonlinear, rational, and executable primary-care plan is very possible. And this is because our decision engine will use objective measures guided by clinical best practices instead of Giant preferences, which cannot be well coordinated. Your firm may well develop far more sophisticated objective assessment systems than my basic recommendation that follows. But because your firm will want to get started quickly, you'll need to "think big, start small, and move fast." So I recommend that your primary-care assessment systems start simple.

Table 10.1 VMI Calculation

VMI = specialty competence × specialty integration × labor leverage factor

An easy mathematical representation of a client's ability to respond to the competing constraints challenging its value-management capacity should be a good start. This will help us reduce their overall adaptive capacity score to something that we can refer to as the *Value-Management Index* (VMI) for the Everything-Else Department. It can be calculated as shown in Table 10.1.

Specialty Competence

A specialist-competence assessment is easily obtainable by briefly reviewing compliance history in core accounting and information systems functions. Most of us easily know the functional competencies of our clients, because we deal with their output in a pretty intimate way during our compliance work. Quantifying this competency on a scale of one to ten—with ten being the highest degree of competence—will be adequate for our index measurement.

Specialty Integration

The ability to seamlessly integrate various specialist functions into a system that continuously produces transparent and relevant information is easily estimated by mapping all costs of the Everything-Else Department chronologically, including those spent on services to your firm. In a well-integrated specialist environment, costs are incurred at a steady pace. There are minimal cost bulges, because allocative efficiency is driving costs toward the place where value is created and taking them from places where they don't create value.

In a poorly integrated Everything-Else Department, you'll observe blips on the cost curve around the end of both periodic earning cycles and outside of high-activity sales and production cycles. This lack of integration indicates an operational environment where important informational needs are only dealt with "when we're not quite so busy" or "when we have the time." Again, a one-to-ten scale will work nicely.

Labor Leverage Factor

At this point, your client will have an intermediate VMI of between one and one hundred. If we only had those two variables to deal with in our assessment, our primary-care exam would be pretty tidy. But having an Everything-Else Department that can handle the nature and extent of today's transactional environment isn't really adequate to the value-management needs of our globally integrating economy any longer. Because of this reality, we also must assess our clients' ability to cost-effectively adapt to the future demands of the markets for their inputs and outputs.

The concept of scalability, both quantitative and qualitative, will need to be incorporated into the VMI to have a complete assessment that our cooperating specialists can use to make group and individual recommendations. Adding this last factor will put our cooperating specialists in a position to complete the value-management assessment of not only their clients' "good" and "better" value-management capabilities, but their "best."

It is this "best" value-management system that has the high degree of flexibility needed to quickly reallocate funds to appropriate new services as new capabilities are demanded by the marketplace. This scalability can be measured as the percentage of human-capital costs incurred for fully employed labor in the Everything-Else Department compared to total human capital costs incurred, whether contracted or employed, including expenditures on your firm's services.

For example, an enterprise that fully employs most of its specialist labor suffers from a low degree of adaptability to change. That's because laying off full-time employees to hire people with new abilities is a painful, expensive process. For good reasons, layoffs generally occur only as a last resort after having explored all other options. The downside to this is that such a company can only respond very slowly to the allocative efficiency demands of the economy.

Alternatively, if all specialist labor is not employed permanently, but outsourced to a contract infrastructure provider, the adaptability score is very high. Redeployment of labor costs can happen quickly because they're not employed. The scale of this factor is set as zero to one, with one being the most adaptable and zero being the least adaptable Everything-Else-Department scalability.

Value-Management Index

We've now quantified our client's ability to cost-effectively adapt to the economy's need for relevance, transparency, and an array of choices. We can now ask our nonlinear (but uniform) decision engines to help instruct us individually and as a group on how to proceed with a growth-oriented and outcome-focused client development plan. This simple equation yields an effective algorithm for the instructions about which professional competencies to apply to which aspect of client needs and when to do so.

Returning to our nonprofit example of Chapter 6, for example, if I had assessed this client's VMI before engaging him originally, I might have assessed it something like what is presented in Case No. 1 (see Table 10.2). Out of a potential score of 100, this result is pretty dismal. But looking at the underlying factor scores, there's hidden guidance about what to do about it. The scores for competence and labor leverage are actually not bad at all. It's that dreadful integration factor of four out of ten that's dragging the score down. Alternatively, for example, one could arrive at the same VMI with the following calculation for Case No. 2 (see Table 10.3). Despite the VMI being exactly the same score, the decision tree you'd devise from this formula would lead to two different avenues of investigation. The first, which is our nonprofit client case study, indicates a need to look into process integration, or our primary-care numerator. Specialty competence in both instances is measured as a constant at a score of eight. Typically, our specialist-care practitioners would be able to recognize and respond to that need.

Table 10.2 VMI Indicating Value Deficit

VMI =	specialty competence × specialty integration × labor leverage factor
=	8 × 4 × 0.9
=	28.8

Table 10.3 VMI Indicating Cost Overrun

VMI =	specialty competence × specialty integration × labor leverage factor
=	8 × 9 × 0.4
=	28.8

But the low integration score of our nonprofit client indicates a transparency problem. Specialist competency and relevance were just fine. Our audit, tax, and financial services professionals were able to tell our client exactly what went wrong during the previous year, the time that our client representatives were making their choices. Unfortunately, the timing of the presentation of that audit and tax information was way too far in the future to be useful to the executive function's decision-making processes, so it didn't meet our transparency requirement.

In our theoretical Case No. 2, the exact same VMI score of 28.8 indicates not primarily a transparency problem, but an Everything-Else Department that's either vastly overpriced or suffering relevance problems or engineering risks that affect its scalability. We don't know which right now, but we don't need to know that in the primary-care assessment phase.

What we do need to know is what our next process step is as a team so that we can drill down to the root of the client need as efficiently as possible. Despite the complexity of completely diagnosing and treating our client condition, it doesn't require that all of your practitioners file into a meeting to react to client needs as a team. Each of us simply needs to have a small universe of information and decision-making possibilities to know what action to take, whether that action is to continue with a particular treatment plan or make a referral.

We could make a graph that gives us something of a picture of the three-dimensional universe of costs and the degrees of specialization, labor leverage, and integration present to illustrate how awfully complex our treatment possibilities are. I toyed briefly with doing just that, until I realized there might be three people in the world who really wanted to ponder that graph. And I was one of them.

So I took the good advice from Ideo's Tim Brown about the dangers of top-down, grand-style design thinking with busy, but now cooperating, specialist practitioners who used to get to be Giants. All they really want to know is that their specialist contribution is faithfully and competently executed so that they can get on to the next important task in their specialist practices. They want to know the next step in the process.

And because our VMI calculation contains more than one variable, it necessarily generates an algorithm that considers and accommodates all of them. It's only with the help of such decision engines that we can efficiently guide a group of individual cooperating specialists to the next step in complex processes involving many other specialists but with minimal group consultation.

These pristinely uniform but nonlinear processes will help us address unique client needs as a group. Far from being designed to accommodate specialist mills producing marketplace commodities, these processes are designed to produce valuable outcomes that arise from unique client conditions.

Referral to Nowhere

It certainly can't have escaped notice that at some point our cooperating specialists might need to refer a client to another specialist in your firm based on need. Our constraints analysis is telling us that knowing which one of those specialists to refer to will become increasingly difficult. As we chop information system components into smaller and smaller bits and staff them with less and less labor, each component of that system will have a shrinking exposure to all the others. Information systems will suffer greater integration problems.

If each one of our specialists had intimate knowledge of all of our other specialists' competencies, referral would be easy. Unfortunately, this is not always the case. And sadly, the phenomenon of specialist disconnection from one another's competencies is painfully reflected in a correspondingly painful disconnection of those practitioners from the growth strategies of their firms.

The ability to know where to send our illustrative nonprofit client cannot be reduced to a single step in a linear process, much as we'd like it to be. Sometimes there will be multiple possibilities in the decision trees of our practice algorithm, and our own special areas of study won't be adequate to refine a diagnosis. The relative balance of VMI formula variables will yield subtle diagnostic differences that some of us may not have the training or experience to assess.

So it should be no surprise that we'll need a new specialty in our profession—whether we call it CFO Advisory Specialist, Integration Specialist, Melancon's XYZ credential from 2001 (see Chapter 11), Family Practice Accountant, or Internist. It's pretty clear, when we compare the resources available in our firms today to the economy's growing value demands, that we need to create a new integration specialty competent to help guide outcomes in a world of complex inputs.

It was the disappearance of the original Finder Giants that gave rise to the introduction of salespeople as the technology boom began to shrink (and functionally specialize) our profession's population along with all of its support functions. This loss, and the resulting adaptive response, had the effect of defining the strategy of our growth needs during the last quarter century. We had a "sales problem." It didn't really matter what we were selling, we simply needed more of it. Our Finders had gone missing.

Today, the imminent departure of our Minder Giants is about to create a similar defining moment. As our value creators depart and are unable to leave the keys to the value-creation car to a new generation of cheap, generally skilled labor, the emerging imperative that will drive growth and profitability for the next quarter century will be value management. And that future profitability, far from being contained in labor pyramids, will depend on our ability to manage value as a team in increasingly complex and rapidly changing environments.

As we approach the inevitable day when integration specialists arrive in our firms, we'll serve ourselves well to be prepared for them. The Days of the Giants lurk too recently in our past to easily leave behind the specialist fear of having the Finders and Minders replaced by a newer and even more fearsome breed of Giants to whom they must be subservient. Accordingly, we must first prepare our good Mayo Clinic practice foundation of teamwork, collegiality, professionalism, and respect. Then, rather than being a superman consultant leveraging every mere technician in his wake, our new integration specialty will be revealed to be a humble servant of clinical governance responsible for organizing our specialist-care best practices into a primary-care value stream.

Chapter 11

The New Minders

Designing and implementing a clinical governance system that could marry the market's demand for outcomes and the New Giants' need to lead value creation in their own practices was essential groundwork. Without that system, our practitioners would have no way of knowing what to do with their patients, other than conducting their own specialist procedures and sending them home to recover. The old system of Minder Giant governance just wasn't going to be adequate to cost-effectively address the value-creation challenge any longer.

And the algorithms—our decision engines—that will allow those cooperating specialists to accomplish that renewed mission together are no less critical. Without a common, evidence-based language to communicate among themselves, our increasingly isolated specialist practitioners would have no way to efficiently meet those market demands as a group. To prevent creating an environment of "death by meeting," our highly competent specialists need those decision engines to efficiently do the right thing by their patients so that they can then quickly get on with their specialist rounds.

But the implementation of the Days of the New Giants won't be complete without one last step, and it's not a small one. In fact, it's a rather big one. As our Minder Giants of yesterday's value-creation systems begin to take their well-deserved retirements, we need to find a way to create a new specialty that replaces their integration function. It won't be easy, and it will take some time.

A helpful way to think about this is contained in our medical-practice analogy. The medical profession had Giants, too, and they needed to make the move from the old ones to the new ones as the market's demands for medical specialization and patient outcomes competed with one another. Finally, in 1969, family medicine was formally recognized as a medical specialty as a way to adapt to those demands. General practitioners of the day were allowed to be grandfathered into that system, but the profession abolished the practice of allowing only one year of residency for general practice after medical school.

Today, nearly a half century after that movement, it's pretty easy to see our own challenge. We need to replace our departing Minder Giants and, like any model, the newer one will be more specialized than the older one. Unfortunately, this critical adaptation arises right at the time that we don't have a lot of extra profitability to invest in operational capability. Its success will depend entirely on group cooperation, lean operations in our specialist silos, and a means-of-the-mission befitting the coming value-management challenge. Times are tough.

Fortunately for our New Giants, they'll have already laid the groundwork for this reality by instituting our Chapters 5 and 6 price–value monitoring mechanisms designed to respond to the world economy's competing constraints. Before making any investment in our primary-care numerator by adding an integration specialty, we wisely began monitoring and controlling our specialist-care denominators to pay for this important cost migration. Our New Giants know that they must maintain equilibrium between specialist-care costs and outcome-based, primary-care value.

Melancon's Undiscovered General Practitioner

Over ten years ago, Barry Melancon, president and CEO of the American Institute of Certified Public Accountants (AICPA), proposed an initiative to create a new credential. It was to be a global, multidisciplinary one that would emphasize complex problem solving through the integration of specialist disciplines such as accounting, law, insurance, organizational development, finance, human resources, and information technology. The credential would not be exclusive to the CPA profession, because all the underlying multidisciplinary tools were not provided by us.

Melancon believed that despite the originating view of the CPA credential as a diverse one that would allow for the development of this multidisciplinary function as a matter of best practices, modern CPA candidates were being forced to pass through the eye of the needle in their training and experience through increasing pressure to specialize. His conclusion was that a new credential was needed to deliver what the national and international business community was clamoring for. That community wanted business professionals with the knowledge and experience necessary to apply comprehensive business solutions to complex problems using any or all of the disciplines identified previously.

In the October 2001 *Journal of Accountancy,* Jim Emerson,* a leading industry analyst, published an open letter to our profession in support of Melancon's XYZ credentialing initiative. It reads in part:

> Since 1993, we have talked to approximately 15,000 major U.S.-based companies about their views on global professional services. Several common themes have emerged from many of these interviews. One is the reality that even the world's largest companies do not have the capability or desire to integrate the various disciplines necessary to get many jobs done. *At a minimum, most clients believe it is the job of the service provider to integrate their own competencies* [emphasis added] and, ideally, to also integrate services from third parties to deliver comprehensive solutions.

Unfortunately, the XYZ project was an ambitious and visionary effort that was doomed to fail. By a two-to-one margin, the membership voted down the proposal to proceed with the project. Melancon's effort to begin preparing to replace our retiring Minder Giants with the integrator position suffered from the understandable political flaw of being a bit before its time in our profession's development to gain acceptance.

The primary concern expressed by practitioners at the time was about the potential for the degradation of the CPA brand. There has always been resistance in our profession to the granting of specialist credentials because of the belief that such designation would dilute or devalue the importance of the original CPA certificate. This might be analogous to a physician of a century ago fearing that the MD brand would be diluted by the granting of a dermatology specialty credential. Like most fears, this one, too, defies rational thinking and is plainly unsupportable.

But such a discussion about ourselves and our credentials in professional circles today reveals powerful fears at the root of the rejection of Melancon's proposal. Our history as competitive generalists, each of us striving to

---

* Emerson, Jim. "The XYZ Credential: An Opportunity to Lead the Professional Services Industry in the 21st Century." *Journal of Accountancy*, October 2001.

remain as one of the dying breed of Giants, is a story of practitioner-on-practitioner operational leverage that ultimately translated into financial leverage. And the Giant-centered output metrics from that competitive landscape still play out, rather unproductively, in all parts of our professional lives today.

Compensation, recognition, status, and feelings of being valued are all intricately intertwined with our sense of professional self. It's a complicated brew that contributes little to our ability to develop into the outcome-producing group of collaborating specialists of the future. Rather than fearing the degradation of our *brand*, we're actually petrified at the thought of the devaluation of *ourselves*, and in a very personal way.

By contrast, we could comfortably rationalize over the last quarter century that, as accountants, we were not well suited to the sales function. The need to hire sales professionals to replace our decommissioned Finder Giants was a natural extension of the specialization constraint. It's best to leave specialist work to those who are qualified, we reasoned.

But the replacement of the Minders would not go so easily.

> You want to replace my Minder Giant's *relationship management* function with a new specialty? That's where I draw the line! No one's going to step into that value-creation role while I'm still showing up at the office! I know the client best. We've known each other for years. How could I possibly want you, Mr. XYZ Credential-fancy-pants with no client history, to provide these integration services to my clients?

It became clear in the failed attempt to create our XYZ practitioner that any credentialing effort of the future intended to train the replacement for the Minder Giants needed to sidestep two important motivational barriers.

The first such barrier is that the Minder Giants didn't want to give up the practice car keys of relationship management to anyone outside of our CPA discipline. XYZ was intended to be a credential that, however rigorous in its requirements, any number of professions could aspire to. And despite the fact that its integration function would be rooted in "evidence management" as opposed to the retiring Minder Giants' "relationship management" job, having anyone but their own CPA brethren in charge of it lacked political support. It smacked of that loss of self-determination that we fear so terribly.

And the second motivational barrier is that we had gradually lost interest in integrating our specialist procedures into our clients' value-creation streams. As our production silos got more linear with each successive year, for efficiency reasons, we began to actually withdraw from the relevance, transparency, and choices infrastructure of the enterprises we served. Integration gradually became the job of our clients' internal CPA colleagues.

We didn't mind managing relationships, because that could be done outside our daily work environments without intersilo interference. Evidence management, on the other hand, would put those linear production environments in harm's way. Everyone at the firm would need to begin responding to their colleagues as a matter of professional duty, each of them spending at least some time every week at the clinic, enforcing the primary-care standards of our clinical governance system. The creation of a position in 2001 that didn't fit our existing operational environments, however visionary and well crafted, made no sense to us.

Taking a long and hard look at that evolutionary hiccup in the Minder replacement process is a fascinating study. Not every CPA in public practice is blessed with the opportunity to sit back and think about such things. Our lives are typically far too busy with the duties of our sacred specialist missions to spend a lot of time with what amounts to professional navel-gazing.

But having taken a leave from active practice to do just that—serve as a paleontologist of sorts for my profession—I thought I should be able to map our lineage in much the same way that we see on those pictures meant to graphically show the history of Ape to Neanderthal to Modern Man. The act of doing so might help me better understand our New Minders—what they look like, what adaptations they'll have made to survive, and when they'll arrive.

The Lineage of the Giants

Table 11.1 illustrates basic business environmental attributes as they existed in the Days of the Giants.

Business model. During the Days of the Giants, accounting was considered to be one of the "named professions," along with medicine, law, engineering, architecture, actuarial science, and others. The definition of what constitutes a professional occupation has properly changed with modern times, but when we thought of the reason for our existence, we didn't intuitively think of it as a business model. When we used the term *professional practice*, we meant it. We always believed that society's need for our services transcended our need to make a living.

Table 11.1   Etiology of the Giants

Attribute	The Days of the Giants
Business model	Professional practice
Service entry point	Procedure
Growth imperative	Value creation
Service integrator	CPA firm
Management system	Hierarchical
Always staffed by a CPA?	Yes

Service entry point. The primary point of entry into our clients' lives—the *channel*, to use a common sales-modeling phrase we employed to establish initial contact with them—was typically a procedure. Financial statements and tax returns were the most common points of original contact, not unlike today.

Growth imperative. It has been known for a long time that there are only just so many tax returns and audits to go around. Those regulatory procedures would never serve as the basis for enough growth to maintain relevance in the economy or for the growth requirements of our firms' ownership continuation. In the Days of the Giants, the growth imperative of value creation kept expanding our profession's deliverables, because we had access to a cheap, generally skilled labor supply. Not only was it easy to create this value, but the succession of that capability—value management—was built into what amounted to a not particularly well-documented, crowd-sourcing effort. All we needed to keep it going was a sufficient body count.

Service integrator. Finder, Minder, and Grinder succession systems flourished during those salad days of our youth. We were more than happy to integrate the services of our firms into our customers' value streams because it was easy to do. All you had to do was listen to what clients told you they needed, and then go back to the office to find a stable of talent ready and willing to service those needs. It was child's play.

Management system. We hear a lot these days about the need to move from hierarchical management systems to collaborative ones. The Giants can view such a need suspiciously, secretly believing that such nonsense is being forced upon us by willful and pampered children who were never taught the value of following orders like we were taught back in the day. Following the orders of the Giants created value back then. Why a cheap and permanent supply of good order-takers won't be serving as the basis for value management in the future is still something of a mystery for some of us.

CPA staffing. Everyone was a CPA in the Days of the Giants. It was the low-watermark for survival in that competitive place. If you were unable to pass the CPA exam, and pass it quickly, it didn't bode well for your employment prospects in public accounting. That phenomenon gradually faded over time, eventually coming to a time when passing the exam not only lost its urgency, but was replaced by a growing ambivalence toward it. But despite the fact that there has been a massive decline in the number of CPAs relative to economic growth, it has happened for three distinct reasons, apathy about the relevance of certification only being one of them:

Unit of output productivity. The reduction in CPA body count that happened because of unit-of-output productivity cannot, and should not, be reversed. It's normal. Computer chips are fast, whereas we were slow. Nothing can change the fact that we can crunch a whole lot more numbers way faster than twenty-five years ago. But now that our New Giants have taken up measuring primary and specialist care efficiency with separate numerators (fair market values) and denominators (costs to produce), they know that unit-of-output productivity is only one measure that we need to consider in assessing efficiency in our professional environment.

Specialization. The part of CPA shrinkage that occurred because of the rise in allied and ancillary services due to specialization is also normal, unavoidable, and actually a good thing. Our increasingly expensive junior colleagues can no longer be sent out on missions to fix bad accounting work and look for value-creation opportunities as a side job. They have specialist procedures to perform. And the specialist mechanics of other Everything-Else-Department services are best left to technical-support professionals trained to perform them efficiently and effectively.

Relevance, transparency, and choices. But the one reason for CPA certification growth decline that we not only can address, but must reverse as a matter of survival of the species, is our declining relevance due to our inability to shift resources quickly enough *away* from earnings and financial position measurement and *toward* relevance, transparency, and choices. That's the part of the Days of the Giants that we must re-create. If we don't, someone else will do it for us, and we can honorably retreat to the battle lines drawn at opinion-giving on earnings and financial position. It's a permanent and honorable place to practice that will continue to shrink in size, however, as the economy allocates resources to value-producing activities.

Exit the Finders

As time progressed on our evolutionary chart, our Finders began giving way to the more upright-walking salesperson. This adaptation to specialization and productivity pressure has been crucial to the growth of accounting firms since the mid-1990s. It was made possible largely because we split our business model into two similar but distinct parts. While we maintained a professional-practice model for our accounting specialists doing their original service-point-of-entry procedures (audits and tax returns), we also began operating sales and production cycles for allied services "right next door" (see Table 11.2).

We weren't always comfortable and could voice our discomfort privately in the context of "independence problems" or "I'm not a salesperson." But looking at it honestly, we relied heavily on our new sales and production cycles to make up for the loss of profitability associated with declining labor leverage that was occurring due to that self-same productivity and specialization. And we could also tolerate it because *absolutely all of the other environmental attributes of our now-bifurcated business model matched up.*

Table 11.2   Etiology of the Giants—Post Finder

Attribute	CPA Procedural Specialists	Product Salesperson
Business model	Professional practice	Sales and production
Service entry point	Specialist procedures	Product
Growth imperative	More specialist procedures	Sell anything
Service integrator	Client	Client
Management system	Hierarchical	Hierarchical
Always staffed by a CPA?	Yes	No

The service entry point was still identical to what it was in the Days of the Giants. Whether it was a tax return, an audit, or the installation of a proprietary hardware or software system, our point of entry was transactional. Outcomes would spring organically from those transactions as cheap, competitive, and generally skilled talent swarmed around them during engagement performance.

And our growth imperative was served organically as well. Sell something. Anything. Do a good job. Earn the right to sell something else. Despite the reality that we were abandoning value creation in favor of a sales-and-production model to serve as the foundation of our growth imperative, excess value was happening automatically due to a significant upward tilt in the technology curve. This resulted in more services to more people, more valuably, and at a declining cost due to unit-of-output productivity gains fueled by a shrinking microchip.

And as long as we kept our procedural silos separate from one another, we could keep our hierarchical management systems on both sides of our split-business model. This linearity was an important operational provision that enhanced our ability to separate ourselves from one another and continue to shrink the specialist-care denominators in our productivity equations. But not only was it an important operational necessity, it was an important philosophical need for our soon-to-be-departing Minder and Grinder Giants. It fit neatly into our narrative that all our junior colleagues really needed was increased accountability to the discipline of a command-and-control system to succeed us. After all, it had worked for us.

But as the growth imperative of selling products and specialist procedures overtook our ability and desire to perform the integration function, it was hard to see the looming catastrophe on the horizon. One unsustainable form of business leverage (cheap labor) was simply replacing another unsustainable form of profitability (commodity service strategy). But the economic bubble phenomenon of the early part of the century had completely masked that sustainability problem.

As a result, the linear production systems that it took to pack more specialist procedures into less time became a more pressing adaptation than finding a cost-effective way to re-create the Days of the Giants. Not only was the expansion of value no longer considered a growth imperative, it had became a wistful memory of an aging population of Minder and Grinder Giants.

So I started pinning Prehistoric Accountant figures on my corkboard to document our adaptive responses to the competition among the various environmental constraints. We'd progressed from the Days of the Giants, a

Table 11.3 Pre and Post Finder Giant Compared

Attribute	The Days of the Giants	CPA Procedural Specialists	Product Salesperson
Business model	Professional practice	Professional practice	Sales and production
Service entry point	Procedure	Specialist procedures	Product
Growth imperative	Value creation	More specialist procedures	Sell anything
Service integrator	CPA firm	Client	Client
Management system	Hierarchical	Hierarchical	Hierarchical
Always staffed by a CPA?	Yes	Yes	No

professional-practice model rooted in crowd-sourced value-creation infrastructure, to the Days of the Microchip, a bifurcated professional practice/sales and production business model, where value management was becoming the job of our clients. And despite the phenomenon of the business environmental attributes in our new split-business model beginning to merge into alignment with one another, they began diverging from the Giants' model in a couple of significant ways (see Table 11.3).

First, despite the fact that the service entry point was transactional, just like before, the professional imperative driving practice growth after completion of that first transaction had changed dramatically. In the Days of the Giants, our creed was: Sell something. Anything. Do a good job. Try to understand the client's needs while you're there. Go back to the office and make a plan to serve those needs. The Giants' growth imperative was outcome based despite the original point-of-service entry being transactional (audits and tax returns).

Second, the New Giants began giving up the service-integration function to our internal client representatives as a matter of specialist care "efficiency." As specialization, unit-of-output productivity, and allocative efficiency combined to squeeze us and our pricing, we gradually abandoned the desire and ability to perform the integration function at all, much to the dismay of our declining population of Giants. And talk of commoditization increased along with a growing sense, voiced in the narrative of the Days of the Giants, that our successors were failing us despite the fact that they were doing exactly what we asked them to do: Specialize and work faster.

It was clear now that the two practice model elements—(1) the nature of our growth imperative and (2) who should integrate our services into the value stream of our clients' lives—were coming into alignment on both sides of our bifurcated business model. They were in agreement with one another in that the goal was to provide more services to more people at a declining cost. Unfortunately, though, both of those model elements now disagreed with the original proposition of the Giants, which was to perform those procedures more valuably.

Exit the Minders

The CPA profession now had a serious problem. Its labor leverage, the original foundation of equity succession, was disappearing. In addition to that, the rising commoditization of all of its procedural work—gradually at first and then, suddenly, with the Great Recession—meant that the growth imperative founded in "selling more stuff" wasn't going to be able to fill the profitability gap any longer. Something would have to be done to restore a growth imperative founded in the ability to create the value that the marketplace was demanding.

The first attempt to do so arrived in 2001 with Melancon's proposal of the XYZ credential. Similar to a consulting model based on lean operations, it comprehensively addressed our profession's business model by taking into account all of the important intervening environmental adaptations. The XYZ credential appeared to line up perfectly with us and our market's needs and, perhaps just as important, with the narrative of the Days of the Giants (see Table 11.4).

Our service entry point would need to change from one of procedures to outcomes. The New Giants were discovering that their transactional experts were getting so focused on their specialist procedures that outcome-based needs were being overlooked. And even when those outcome-based needs were known, we often lacked an effective way to integrate our products to address those needs. But with a service entry point based on outcomes, we could now design and operate such systems.

Reviving the growth imperative of value management in public accounting—value creation, but with the now-necessary non-labor-dependent succession capability—would bring the integration function firmly into the hands of qualified specialists trained for it. And it would give public

Table 11.4   Giants and XYZ Compared

Attribute	The Days of the Giants	XYZ Credential (2001)
Business model	Professional practice	Professional practice
Service entry point	Procedure	Outcome
Growth imperative	Value creation	Value management
Service integrator	CPA firm	CPA firm
Management system	Hierarchical	Collaborative
Always staffed by a CPA?	Yes	No

accounting firms the important opportunity to regain the preeminence they enjoyed back in the Days of the Giants.

Surely our partner groups in public accounting would aggressively compete with professionals in other disciplines for the opportunity to be the best at this new function. It was, after all, merely intended to re-create the capabilities and status that we'd already enjoyed in the Days of the Giants. All we had to do was to introduce a position that would serve as the New Minder, set her free among our brave new population of collaboration-prone Gen X through Z colleagues, and stand back to watch the future unfold. Unfortunately, human nature interfered in a rather predictable way.

The existing Minder Giants, closing in on their well-earned retirements, really didn't want to think about new credentials and duties and expertise to replace something they already knew how to do. They knew how to manage relationships and didn't want to think about managing evidence of business health instead. It wasn't a glaring emergency yet, and it sounded risky. But not only did they not want to do the new integration work themselves, *they didn't want any another profession to do it for them.*

Allowing someone outside of what we saw as our profession's natural domain to "manage evidence" with respect to our clients' process infrastructures sounded like we would lose the relationship preeminence that we relied upon to feel secure in our business dealings. Our departing Minders would have no part in approving a position that could usurp the customer-relationship primacy they enjoyed in serving clients.

The XYZ credential died the understandable death of being a job description in search of a professional-practice model that hadn't yet been designed or deployed. Despite this, the value-management needs of the economy were only going to get more pressing over the course of the next decade. We would need to deal with that reality soon.

The next adaptive response arrived at the beginning of 2012. The AICPA, in cooperation with the Chartered Institute of Management Accountants in the United Kingdom, began offering a credential to their memberships called the Chartered Global Management Accountant (CGMA) designation. This time, however, the adaptation was designed not only to account for the competition of the market's demand for value, increasing specialization, and the effects of allocative efficiency—but also for the vagaries of human nature that were not so well envisioned during the vetting of the XYZ credential.

During that discussion, we learned that our practitioners were not ready to accept the mantle of the new integration specialty. The integration of all specialties into a value stream via evidence management would require a lot more interpersonal risk than relationship management, which could be accomplished largely outside of the scope of our daily transactional work environment. We didn't want to do anything that would upset the political order of our existing business relationships.

Not only that: Once again, we didn't want anyone doing it for us. Melancon's proposal that XYZ be available to other professions was a complete nonstarter, as our practitioners envisioned shifting alliances that didn't fit with their existing relationship-management universes.

We were more than happy, though, to accept integration direction from our client representatives. After all, we reported to them. Many times they were directly responsible for paying us, so our fear of abandonment could be kept at bay while retaining the professional vision of ourselves as the valuable specialists that we wanted to be. And the adaptation necessary to account for our security needs looked like what is shown in Table 11.5.

The CGMA certification was easily adopted by both memberships (unlike the vote on the original XYZ credential). Our growth imperative could be restored to the Days of the Giants, albeit in modified form because of the realities of specialization and unit-of-output productivity. All we needed to do was to make sure that (1) the integration position was staffed by one of our CPA colleagues in industry and (2) we in public accounting wouldn't have to be that person.

Both our practitioners' needs for security and the economy's needs for value were accounted for through evolutionary adaptation. But I still had the nagging suspicion that I might be congratulating myself too soon on having come to the end of my quest to document the lineage of the Giants—from the old to the new.

Table 11.5   XYZ and CGMA Compared

Attribute	XYZ Credential (2001)	CGMA Credential (2011)
Business model	Professional practice	Professional practice
Service entry point	Outcome	Outcome
Growth imperative	Value management	Value management
Service integrator	CPA firm	Client
Management system	Collaborative	Collaborative
Always staffed by a CPA?	No	Yes

In the last step, I'd only analyzed the failings of the XYZ credential and the adaptation required to create acceptance of the CGMA designation. If the goal was to return again to the Days of the Giants, I wasn't comfortable that I'd yet seen the Promised Land. So I pinned them up together on my corkboard (see Table 11.6).

The Days of the Giants compared favorably to the one where a New Minder position was occupied by the CGMA. This position, now *inside* of our clients' offices—together with good sales teams from outside accounting firms plus many highly trained procedural specialists—would be the core of the value-management engine needed by business in today's global economy. But there were necessary adaptations.

In a world now of increasingly pricey and specialized human resources, we no longer would have the luxury of sending in transactional specialists to lead development of our clients' value-management systems. An outcome-focused service entry point would mean that the CGMA would be the orchestrator of value management in the enterprise. The deployment of our

Table 11.6   Minder Giants and CGMA Compared

Attribute	The Days of the Giants	CGMA Credential (2011)
Business model	Professional practice	Professional practice
Service entry point	Procedure	Outcome
Growth imperative	Value creation	Value management
Service integrator	CPA firm	Client
Management system	Hierarchical	Collaborative
Always staffed by a CPA?	Yes	Yes

procedural specialists in support of decision making by managing relevance, transparency, and choices would now be the province of someone other than those of us who worked in public accounting.

After a hard look at the competing constraints in the economy, we were able to admit that our successors were not spoiled and willful children who needed a collaborative management system because they didn't know how to take orders. Rather, unit-of-output productivity gains and specialization requirements had shrunk and specialized our labor population so much that a hierarchical labor-leverage system was no longer economically viable as a value-management engine.

Sure, we could do it, but not at the prices the economy was willing to pay any longer. Now, we'd need to systematically manage value via process to successfully integrate all of these experts. The Days of the Giants were now officially over because of very real and compelling economic changes, not failed cultural appeals to a new generation.

So, after accounting for the optimization of all the competing economic constraints, everything in a CGMA-led value-management system mirrors the variable inputs, value-managed processes, and expanding outputs of the Days of the Giants. Even though we've conceded that value will be managed by someone inside our clients' offices rather than us, at least that critical job is getting done. The CGMA certification, appropriately aimed at folks with experience in management accounting who are responsible for growth in the economy's decision-support function, is not being forced on our public practitioners.

But we also need to understand—and admit to ourselves—that without the CGMA function (or its equivalent function in public accounting), we don't have any real chance of regaining a growth imperative capable of attracting vast legions of a new generation of professionals to an ever-expanding mission. Without a compelling growth mission that's aligned with the relevance, transparency, and choices infrastructures of the enterprises we serve, our New Giants will continue to abandon public accounting to join someone else who does accept that mission. However, there's no dishonor—professional or personal—in permanently retreating to our specialist silos and abandoning the quest to create the Days of the New Giants.

But there is hope. Inevitably, the final evolutionary step for us to take as a profession is hard-coded into the future by way of continuing specialization and unit-of-output and productivity gains. Just as any specialist function is sourced from outside service providers today for scalability reasons, so, too, will the CGMA position continue in its productivity climb. Eventually (very soon, actually), it will be very common to have this important function

Table 11.7 Projected arrival of the New Giants

Attribute	The Days of the Giants	CGMA Credential (2011)	The New Giants
Business model	Professional practice	Professional practice	Professional practice
Service entry point	Procedure	Outcome	Outcome
Growth imperative	Value creation	Value management	Value management
Service integrator	CPA firm	Client	CGMA sourced from CPA firm
Management system	Hierarchical	Collaborative	Collaborative
Always staffed by a CPA?	Yes	Yes	Yes

purchased from accounting firms just like tax, audit, internal audit, payroll, or any other specialist role in an enterprise (see Table 11.7).

This happy reality will deliver us—albeit very possibly kicking and screaming—to the Days of the New Giants. As the friction between specialization and the economy's demand for value in the form of processes that produce outcomes intensifies, the economy will yield our New Minders as a by-product of that competition. And it will happen whether our profession pursues the opportunity enthusiastically or not.

So Now What?

So it's a valid question to ask whether we should bother establishing the position of the New Minders today. Our succession-implementation journey so far has taught us that there's a specific sequence of cost-effective firm development that's dictated by causality. In the not-too-distant past, we believed that if we could just solve the generational commitment problem by being more culturally responsive and, at the same time, enforcing greater accountability in our outdated hierarchical management silos (a neat trick), then value creation would take care of itself. We now more correctly understand that the reverse is true—that gaining the commitment of our successors depends on rebuilding the value-management mission of our profession.

So training our New Minders today—whether XYZ, CGMA, or lean consultant—would be premature if we didn't have a functioning clinic ready for them to use. Deploying an integration specialist to serve as an evidence manager among procedural specialists not professionally bound by a commitment to a common set of primary-care standards would earn us only the confusion, division, and resentment of our already overburdened practitioners—and not outcomes for our clients.

And there's no way we can build that clinic without lean operations in our current production systems. Any attempt to create something as complex and nonlinear as a clinical governance system—constructed to adequately serve our primary-care standards—without lean mechanisms firmly in place—would burn to the ground in a hail of new non-value-added costs. The fate of "death by meeting" awaits anyone who tries to do so without proper guidance.

And we also know now that we can't realistically institute lean operational environments without making the *three critical market commitments* that will serve as the cultural foundation for future practice:

- A commitment to practitioner-led value creation
- Adaptation to the economy's definition of value
- A professional obligation to pursue transparency, relevance, and choices as the primary mission of accountancy

To us, it would feel like a loss in quality without the support of those principles as we shift resources into the transactional stream of our clients where value lives today—toward relevance, transparency, and choices.

Training and deployment of our New Minders will take a lot of preparatory groundwork. And we now know that we cannot build our new primary-care teams without them.

Chapter 12

Your Primary-Care Teams

Dr. Nicholas LaRusso, the Mayo Clinic's director of the Center for Innovation, has made it very clear that Mayo is profoundly committed to driving value in the delivery of its services. And he's been equally clear in his assertion that this value will be led by Mayo's primary-care teams. The intent is not to downgrade specialization, but to acknowledge that extracting greater outcome-based value from specialist procedural practice requires integration.

After taking a balanced look at the competition of specialization and the demand for outcomes in the marketplace, we know this is no less true for us. Devising a plan to define, assemble, and deploy these primary-care teams will be tricky business, even if we've faithfully prepared our firms with the proper cultural foundation, lean operational environments, and clinical governance systems.

Paradoxically, your "We're going to create more value" declaration in firm leadership meetings conjures up the most negative responses from the very folks you intend to receive the greatest benefit. No matter how you say it, your practitioners will hear "more work." It's a reasonable assumption—lean theory and practice notwithstanding—that if we're not creating enough value today, that doing so tomorrow will require greater effort.

And that same message placed in your firm's brochures will fall on deaf ears in the marketplace as well—dismissed as marketing fluff. It stands to reason that if you've struggled up until now to provide your services "more valuably," you're going to need to quickly establish credibility with the consuming public that your primary-care teams are capable of moving the value ship in the right direction.

So to make immediate, quantifiable progress with which you can create and grow a value-management contract between provider and consumer, your primary-care teams will want to follow a specific quick-start recipe for implementation:

- Establish a simple input metric to measure team cohesion.
- Establish your primary-care teams cross-organizationally.
- Assess your client's Value-Management Index (VMI) and refer the results to your New Minder.

A Simple Measure

One way to think about the balance of quality as we define it in our specialties (correctness, completeness, and precision in an environment of certainty) and how consumers define it (relevance, transparency, and choices in a world of uncertainty) is to express it as a ratio. In the denominator is what we'll refer to as *procedural quality*, and in the numerator we'll measure something called *experienced quality*.

One way to refer to interteam communications about these differing forms of quality is "high value" for experienced quality and "low value" for procedural quality. Before you throw rocks at the design guy, consider an analogy to help better understand that reference from a consumer's standpoint. Let's recall for a moment the story of the Walmart-based eye doctor.

The pricing policy at this particular Walmart is to charge about a hundred dollars for the services of the eye doctor, and you've dutifully submitted to his expert exam. Now imagine that after meeting with the doctor, you were to receive a half dozen phone calls within the next few days from his office asking you for additional information or to stop in for further testing. All you wanted was eyewear that would look good and help you see better, but apparently there's more to it than you imagined. And so you comply.

As a consumer, it's easy to see that additional contacts about the procedure itself are irritating and are actually reducing value in the consumer's eyes. You're a buyer now and can't imagine why this person would need such apparently irrelevant information to get you your glasses. And on top of it all, the cost of the doctor is rising along with each value-killing inquiry.

If, on the other hand, the doctor's technicians were calling about additional eyewear styles that just became available, or new lens production techniques that improve the vision experience, you might actually appreciate the calls. Such calls offer greater transparency of relevant information for you to use in making your choices. But we can also think of it in depressingly familiar form: what this phenomenon looks like in the daily practice life of a CPA.

I was visiting recently with a client of our firm after starting my book-writing hiatus. As I was exchanging pleasantries with a senior accounting department employee, an exasperated staff member looked up from his desk to ask her a question. He'd been asked by a staff member of the accounting firm to produce the balance of a particular loan projected two years out into the future.

"What do they need *this* for?" he asked in obvious frustration. I could tell he was very busy and viewed the staff member's inquiry as an impediment to his getting his real job done. It didn't seem relevant to anything he could imagine. Undoubtedly it had procedural relevance—current maturities of long-term debt or some other amortization exercise—to something that the outside accountants were working on, but that didn't make it any easier to accept.

It was another case of an inquiry intended to create procedural value that was being pursued with a low-value contact. So when we use the shorthand "high value" and "low value," we can understand what we're really talking about. We won't be offended that someone might be viewing our work as irritating and irrelevant even though our intent, planning, and execution are all unswervingly aimed at the highest of quality standards that sometimes only we, as professionals, understand. We can sympathize because when we consume services, we feel exactly the same way.

The ratio of high-value to low-value contacts is a fabulous, easily implemented input metric system that will simultaneously demonstrate to both sides of the value-management contract that you're serious about treating their resources carefully—your practitioners' time and your clients' money. But even beyond instant credibility with quality-conscious specialists and sometimes value-starved clients, there's an even more important motivational reason for wanting to measure and target better performance in this statistic.

The primary-care teams you deploy will need that measuring stick to bind them together in common motivational purpose. There's no lean environment I know of that envisions an endless stream of team meetings about client aches and pains to maintain value-creation traction. Those were the methods and means of the Giants, and we don't have the money to run these antiquated systems any longer. All of your primary-care team members need unfettered access to relevant information to adequately serve their decision-making needs, just like anyone else in the economy. And this ratio is a quick and accessible way for all members of the team to measure traction without stopping to consult one another.

If your firm has a customer-relationship management system, then it's uniquely positioned to begin measuring this vital information. Today it's not untypical for firms to use these technology-based systems to accumulate information about the high-value opportunities evolving in the lives of their clients by monitoring high-value contacts. But perhaps an even more important use for this tool is to record all low-value contacts first, so we can make a plan to eliminate them!

This is because your customers are accumulating information, too. And if a major part of their relationship with you is mired in low-value contact, they'll generally conclude that you won't be able to deliver on new opportunities any more valuably than you could with their audits and tax returns. This isn't an unreasonable conclusion for them to make based on the evidence. What you might have to say that contradicts that evidence will come off as sales puffery.

So establishing an input metric system for the integration of your firm's services gives the team something to accomplish together. Not only do they get to accomplish it together as a team, but it's something both they and their customers want equally. With the powerful evidence of a growing high-value contact ratio, our primary-care teams will remain motivated and connected to the mission.

Cross-Organizational Teams

One of my first direct encounters with the full breadth of what will be the domain of our primary-care team responsibilities was at a client's office, where I found myself interviewing the controller about his function. The company's new owner wanted an overview of the business process infrastructure of the enterprise. Determining the scope of the assessment was at the core of our first meeting, so I asked the controller for a high-level description of his duties.

He began by drawing three squares on the back of a piece of paper. "Around here we're organized like this," he said. "We have sales, production, and everything else." As he finished labeling the three organizational boxes, he paused for dramatic effect. Then he pointed at the box he'd dubbed "everything else" and asserted, "I'm in charge of everything else."

It was an honest and true assessment of his role at the company. Until that point, I hadn't really been able to verbalize what seemed to be the accidental domain of the accounting function—the Everything-Else Department. Now I had a name for this disparate hodgepodge of functions that fell outside the core competencies of the business. In his particular case, "everything else" included:

- Accounting and information management
- Technology
- Human resources
- Payroll and employee benefits administration
- General administration

It was a rather expansive set of core competencies, and I got the strong sense that it was his turf and I was not to presume to pick it apart. He was its Minder Giant.

Historically, as a client-service partner of my CPA firm, I typically would have arrived to establish a connection with him in pursuit of a productive business relationship between our two departments. I was the Minder Giant of Team CPA Firm, and he was the Minder Giant of Team Client. Each of us would have had a labor pyramid behind us that would interact at our ad hoc direction to accomplish the goals of Team Everything-Else Department.

But this time it felt different. The new business owner hadn't sent me there to establish this hierarchical political arrangement as it typically existed between an accounting firm and a potential client. I was being asked to evaluate something that didn't exist on paper—the combined cost-effectiveness of the cross-organizational team created by the current accounting firm and the client's internal staff.

I didn't have a VMI score system at the time to help me assess that cost effectiveness. Contained inside that VMI score—and the relative weight of each component—I could have quickly scored not only specialist competence, but also the cost-effective integration among those specialties. Further, I could have scored the degree of scalability of the entire business process system as reflected in its ratio of employed-to-contracted labor.

But not only didn't I have that analytical tool at my disposal, I didn't have a New Minder back at the office to refer them to. In order for me to proceed with recommending a treatment plan that was directly responsive to the unique nature of their value-management deficit, I'd need these new tools. So in the absence of that, I defaulted to what any underqualified generalist Minder Giant would do: Interview team members from both organizations about their functions and duties so I could build an organizational chart that showed the composition of that broader team.

What I found was unsurprising. What used to be a whole lot of generally skilled accounting department labor leverage was now flattened to a small population of specialists. Everyone—including the representatives of the outside accounting firm—reported to the Minder Giant that I'd interviewed. He was in charge of the Everything-Else Department.

What impressed me the most was the cooperative nature of all of the team members as they worked together. Our Minder Giant had clearly established his leadership and very effectively laid out the department's goals and means. There was no friction created by an interorganizational interface that needed to be opened and closed every time resources needed to be moved across the team, whether they were employed by the client or the accounting firm. Everyone knew what they needed to accomplish and what tools to use.

It made me think back to team-building situations in my own practice life where things didn't go so well. In poorly led cross-organizational teams, members questioned one another's actions—"What do they need that for?"—instead of fulfilling information requests routinely, and even enthusiastically, as a means to pursue joint accomplishment. Almost every interaction seemed to require an escalation to some level of supervisory involvement. Minor failures in ministerial duties became irritants or, worse, evidence of malfeasance.

But this team functioned seamlessly under the leadership of the lone Minder Giant at the client facility. By drawing the primary-care team lines across both organizations and then leading to that structure, he'd automatically neutralized the vast majority of what could have been low-value contacts.

Unlike a specialist vendor asking a buyer's primary-care team members for follow-up analysis—much like our Walmart eye doctor calling for more information, or our exasperated accounting department employee asking, "What do they want this for?"—these cross-organizational primary-care team members treated one another like stakeholders in a jointly held mission.

But while the input metric of the ratio of high-value to low-value contacts is an important measure of team member commitment, it's not a good measure of the output metric of cost-effectiveness. Simply converting non-value-added activities from high-conflict events to team-neutral events doesn't accomplish efficiency in any lean sense of the word. But it does establish a team environment where non-value-added costs can be examined in a blameless environment. And *that* is critical to the success of your primary-care teams.

A lean-process friend of mine illustrated the difference between input and output metrics using a baseball analogy. After nine innings, the only output metric that means anything is runs scored. Your team needs to score more runs than its opponent to win the game. But during the game, a good way to measure the likelihood of ending the game in that condition is through things like the input metrics of, say, on-base and slugging percentage.

No team ever won a baseball game with on-base statistics. But motivating team members to perform well with regard to them increases the team's chances of ending the game with more runs. In our Everything-Else-Department case, the end of the game is still a long way off. The final output measure of cost-effective performance in our business-process infrastructures includes a lot more than having denizens of that place all playing nice in the sandbox. But we can rest assured that if they're not, we most certainly won't win the game.

The rallying cry that we hear the loudest as our Giants' value-creation methods fade into history is for increased accountability to those declining systems in the hope of regenerating them. But drawing the boundaries of your primary-care teams across all involved organizations, and then establishing a clear input metric like high- to low-value contact, is not an accountability measure for team members.

Rather, it's a permanent, continuous indicator of leadership's commitment to those teams' success. Our new social contract of relevance, transparency, and choices will remain as marketing fluff until our practitioners know that their leadership is committed to their quest of reducing and eliminating costs that do not increase value in the economy. Because while disconnected, overworked, and sometimes downright frightened team members worry about their own individual performance statistics and their place in the batting order, it's the leader's job to keep them focused positively on team goals. Each of them is pursuing the collaboratively held goal of ending the game with the most runs by applying their unique contributions to the group whether on the mound, in the outfield, or at home plate.

The VMI Challenge—Relationships or Evidence?

Very soon now, right around the corner in fact, the measure of how we'll sustain organizational connectedness with our clients will not be founded in the numbers of activities involving human beings—the way we used to measure them. Rather, such connectedness will be based on our ability to consistently and cost-effectively deliver increasing value to the marketplace. And our ability to do that will be pursued less and less through activity management in pursuit of fostering better interpersonal relationships—or relationship management as we think of it now—and increasingly through evidence management in pursuit of healthier clients.

As relationship management that relies on Minder Giant mutual agreement fades into history, the rise of evidence management as the preferred tool to set and maintain organizational connectedness will not change the fundamental nature of how people interact. No new generation of professionals, whichever letter we assign to them, will be able to cast off the shackles of neediness to become a new race of automatons blindly making efficiency recommendations that are indifferent to human wants and needs. People will always respond to one another in ways that are fundamentally driven by the need for relatedness and growth—but only within the economic constraints that limit their process choices.

An easy way to think about what constrains us in our daily lives is to describe our process choices in terms of their variability. In the Days of the Giants, we enjoyed almost unlimited variability in our process choices because of our low-input variability—our cheap, generally skilled labor supply. Clients, too, enjoyed an environment of unlimited outcomes—or high-output variability—as our Finder Giants roamed the halls looking for needs they could promise to fill with their capable, creative, and motivated charges.

As our input variability began to rise through specialization, our response was to lower the amount of variability in our process choices to account for the rise in the cost of our labor—not an unsound choice if it weren't for that pesky world economy and its own rising need for output variability. The post–Great Recession business environment has made it clear that customers expect us to be more valuable to them, all while continually reducing our costs.

As that new economy emerges with the unavoidable twin horizons of rising input and output variability—that is, more expensive and specialized practitioners and the economy's greater outcome demands—we're faced with what seems like an impossible choice. We're being asked to increase our process variability at the same time! And the only realistic way for us to do that is through professionally organized, measured, and targeted means. Our Minder and Grinder Giants are leaving soon, and trying to replace them is no longer a sound strategy.

But still, the notion of assessing a client's VMI and then proceeding with recommendations based on a unique VMI profile seems rather presumptuous as a first step to establishing a client relationship. Intuitively, we balk at the notion of not first establishing a personal relationship with the Minder Giant and then getting permission to assess facts and make recommendations. After all, relationships among human beings are political. On the other hand, evidence is factual, and we could quickly run afoul of the political machinery that got us to the table in the first place.

Having played the relationship-management game myself for a quarter century, I'm no stranger to the risks involved. One needs to be tactful in delivering information that might run counter to management philosophy and practice. And we all know that giving group advice to try to elevate our firms' business-to-business value-management relationship—to become their clinic of choice, if you will—comes at the risk of our own status in the political order.

But we can't let this stop us and our firms from pursuing our professional duty to make an assessment and treatment plan for the relevance, transparency, and choices infrastructure of our patients. It's our sacred duty—and one we can't avoid by ignoring the fact that our clients often engage in the business equivalent of smoking, overeating, not getting enough exercise, and making other generally terrible business lifestyle choices.

So what the VMI assessment helps our teams do now, rather than relying solely on what our patients tell us about themselves—like a good Minder Giant would do—is to increasingly begin basing our recommendations on what we observe about them as well-trained, collaborative professionals. It's the right thing to do. And just as important, it's the water our new fish-practitioners need to successfully and collaboratively lead value management in the future. Stubbornly believing that all we really need to do to restore practitioner accountability is to insist that our New Giants spend more time developing their tree-climbing abilities will not swimmingly yield the results we seek.

So our need to replace the departing Minder Giants with evidence managers puts all of our practitioners on an equal footing. All of them—whether specialty or primary care—will pursue the same goal with the same evidence-management tools. And far from being an entire workforce short of the goal of replicating the business performance of the Days of the Giants, we're actually only one evidence manager and one primary-care team short of having the ingredients to embark on the journey to the Days of the New Giants.

And yet the necessary loss of our role as the conductor of the value-delivery orchestra still strikes paralyzing fear into our hearts. We protect our practice relationships because they're the foundation not just of our incomes, but of our raison d'etre—the very reason for our existence. Sadly, though, there's no super race of business-developing, personal-relationship-usurping, smarter-than-you-are consultants just around the corner that are going to rescue us and our succession systems. It's now time to start building value-management systems for the specialists we've been given rather than waiting for the return of the now-mythical Giants.

So What Now?

Now that we know the foundation for our new value-management systems will not be built through the political negotiation of Giants who command large teams of cheap labor, how do we tell our clients? Will the world economy accept us in our new role? What if we gave a value-management party and nobody showed up?

The reality is that the world economy is demanding it from us, because it's suffering from the same problems we are. An easy way to think about it is to look at the rise of the number of "CXO" positions that are needed by your average Fortune 500 Company. In the not too distant past, it was not uncommon for companies to have a CEO, COO, and CFO. In the simplest form, the latter two reported to the former to create the foundation for a hierarchical management system that easily provided upward accountability mechanisms that fell well within tolerances of effective span-of-control limits.

Today, estimates of the number of CXO functional executive positions run anywhere from ten to as many as seventy-five. This diversity of executive function has obliterated traditional span-of-control theory. Gone are the days when legions of cheap, generally skilled vice presidents competed to make it to the next level of the executive pyramid. Consequently, the role of CEO has shifted dramatically away from the command and control of relatively few functional executives to something else entirely. The retiring Finder, Minder, and Grinder Giants of the world economy are facing the same problems that we are seeing.

I can report to you today that the world economy would love for us to take away the burden of its need to horizontally integrate the core competencies of the Everything-Else Department. And that's because every ounce of an organization's leadership resources consumed in that effort is an ounce less that can be applied integrating its own core competencies in pursuit of fulfilling the social contract that binds its employees, customers, and all other stakeholders.

But despite the obvious critical and universal need for lean-process-improvement engineering in the world economy, its successful implementation is still spotty at best. You can't read a book or an article about process improvement that doesn't contain a major section dedicated to the challenge of creating a permanently self-sustaining improvement culture. In poorly led process-improvement initiatives, the attitude on the shop floor is often, "This too, shall pass," as unwilling participants dig in their heels to wait out the storm.

That's because we human beings have always had a contradictory capacity for pursuing a low-change environment for everyone around us—for our security needs—but at the same time desiring lots of change potential for ourselves, because we want to grow. As leaders—educators, designers, managers, or executives—if we're not careful to balance these two important human needs, which seem to so impossibly compete with one another, we won't be able to sustain continuous improvement. It will be tricky business figuring out how to maximize the security and growth needs of all stakeholders in any social contract.

But despite the seeming impossibility of the task, it has become a challenge we can no longer defer. Leadership's tolerance for negative human-capital fallout related to change management can disappear fast as the fears of how change affects those who play the game—whether it's their status, their pay, or being able to keep their jobs at all—become more compelling to them than any "process improvement" or "value creation" goals they're asked to achieve together. The decision to abandon a process is much easier to make than one to abandon actual people. So we take the easy route.

We need to accept that we can do nothing to prevent the inevitable rise of value management in the world economy. It is being forced on us whether we like it or not. Our only real opportunity is to make things easier on ourselves by embracing it now as the means we'll use to make our lives easier, our jobs and relationships more secure, and the opportunities for rewarding growth more plentiful for us all.

But we cannot do it alone. It will take the commitment of all stakeholders—employees, customers, vendors, shareholders, bankers, government, universities, and many more—to successfully install relevance, transparency, and choices as the definition of the social contract capable of binding all of us together in common purpose. With the foundation of that new contract, we can hope to establish permanent value-management systems that will outperform the Days of the Giants.

But none of those important commitments is likely to take place if we're unable to accept that those days are over because their time has passed. In my own experience—a human-capital environment where the declining narrative of the Days of the Giants subtly told me that our clients didn't value us the way they used to, that our products had become commodities, and that our successors were somehow inadequate to the task at hand—all of this made it easier for me to avoid pointing the finger of blame at myself, where it belonged.

A new leadership narrative, one founded in the proposition that we have *exactly the right people for the times*, is what we need today. That story needs to inspire and motivate the New Giants to provide more services to more people, more valuably, and at a declining cost—not as a distasteful necessity of sustaining the business leverage of the newest owner-class aristocracy, but as a guiding principle of the pursuit of professionalism of the highest order.

With a growth imperative as big as that, and a body of committed specialists united in pursuing it, equity succession will take care of itself.

Bibliography

Brokaw, Tom. *The Greatest Generation*. New York: Dell Publishing, 1998.

Brown, Tim. *Change by Design: How Design Thinking Transforms Organizations and Inspires Innovation*. New York: HarperCollins, 2009.

De Saint-Exupéry, Antoine. *The Wisdom of the Sands*. New York: Harcourt, Brace and Co., 1950.

Dunn, Paul, and Ronald J. Baker. *The Firm of the Future: A Guide for Accountants, Lawyers, and Other Professional Services*. Hoboken, NJ: John Wiley & Sons, 2003.

Emerson, Jim. "The XYZ Credential: An Opportunity to Lead the Professional Services Industry in the 21st Century." *Journal of Accountancy*, October 2001.

Maister, David H. *Strategy and the Fat Smoker: Doing What's Obvious but Not Easy*. Boston: Spangle Press, 2008.

Mayo, William James. Commencement address, Rush Medical College, Chicago, 1910.

Mayo Clinic Model of Care. Mayo Foundation for Medical Education and Research, 2002. http://www.mayo.edu/pmts/mc4200-mc4299/mc4270.pdf.

Ofri, Danielle. "Why Would Anyone Choose to Become a Doctor?" *New York Times Well Blog*, July 21, 2011. http://well.blogs.nytimes.com/2011/07/21/why-would-anyone-choose-to-become-a-doctor/.

Platt Group. "National Benchmarking Report." *Inside Public Accounting*, 2011.

Index

A

Adaptability, 121
Algorithms, practice, 103–104, 111
American Institute of Certified Public
        Accountants (AICPA), 104, 128
Ancillary services of CPA firms, 6

B

Baby boomers, 1
Baker, Ron, 25
Brokaw, Tom, 9
Brown, Tim, 91
Business cycle, 5
Business model, 131

C

Care, standards of. *See* Standards of care
Certified public accountants (CPAs), 2
    brand, value of, 129
    necessity for certificate to practice, 15
    replacement in firms with less expensive
        labor, 5–6
CGMA credential, 140, 141, 143
Change, resistance to, 8
Clinical governance, 111, 119
Collaboration, 95, 96, 103, 108, 138
Commitment, 3, 4–5
Competence. *See* Specialty-competence
        assessment
Competition, 89
    accounting field, in, 2
    human capital, for, 27

Constitution, U.S., 111
Consulting and coaching system, two-track,
        4
Consumers, specialization, role in, 28
Continuity, 78
Cooperation, 110
Core competencies, 80–81
Cost management, 57
Cost-effectiveness, 65
Cross-organizational teams, 148–149
Customer Relationship Manager (CRM), 76
CXO positions, 154

D

Davis-Bacon Act, 95–96, 110
Days of the Giants, 1
Disconnection, 38
Diversity, 15
Dunn, Paul, 25

E

Efficiency, 54
    defining, 58–59
    demands for, 121
Emerson, Jim, 129
Engagement, 55, 56
Enron, 18
Entrepreneurialism, 89
    value of, 94
Experienced quality, 146

159